THE LOST FUTURE

THE LOST FUTURE

AND HOW TO RECLAIM IT

JAN ZIELONKA

YALE UNIVERSITY PRESS
NEW HAVEN AND LONDON

Illustrations courtesy of Andrzej Mleczko

For information about this and other Yale University Press publications, please
contact:
U.S. Office: sales.press@yale.edu   yalebooks.com
Europe Office: sales@yaleup.co.uk   yalebooks.co.uk

Set in Adobe Garamond Regular by IDSUK (DataConnection) Ltd
Printed in Great Britain by TJ Books, Padstow, Cornwall

Library of Congress Control Number: 2022946644

ISBN 978-0-300-26262-9

A catalogue record for this book is available from the British Library.

10 9 8 7 6 5 4 3 2 1

CONTENTS

PREFACE

Are you becoming increasingly frustrated following the political news? Are you concerned about the future of your country, if not the entire planet? Do you think that democracy is underperforming? If so, welcome to the club of anxious and exasperated citizens. It looks as though our politicians are vigorously pursuing new, ambitious agendas, but they are attaining remarkably little. They have acquired extraordinary emergency powers in recent years, can draw upon cutting-edge science, and are utilizing ultra-modern means of communication. However, their hectic work is generating few tangible improvements in our own lives or for the natural environment. Even our favourite politicians, not to mention those we dislike or distrust, are stuck on this hamster wheel. There must be something fundamentally wrong with the democratic political system if we sense that the future is already squandered or even lost. What is it? This book attempts to solve this crucial puzzle. It contends that politics has fallen out of sync with time and space, and it is this failing which largely explains our current inability to secure the future.

Contemporary politics reminds me of a military brass band stuck in traffic during their parade. They continue to march and play, but they are not moving forward. When the music becomes increasingly *vivace*, they intensify their steps, but their rapid movements do not gain any ground. All their efforts seem to be in vain, their fancy uniforms are soaked in sweat, and the musicians' faces reveal a mixture of laughter and despair. The situation looks increasingly absurd.

For my entire life I have been a staunch supporter of democracy, and I am not pleased to see it treading water. When living behind the Iron Curtain in Communist Poland I experienced first-hand how unappealing the alternatives to democracy can be, but not everybody feels the same. In fact, the 2022 Bertelsmann Foundation Index established that for the first time for many years we have now more autocracies in the world than democracies.[1] Presidents Xi Jinping and Vladimir Putin now seem determined to challenge democracies in the military and economic fields. Even in Europe, Australia and North America, politicians willing to sacrifice democracy on the altar of national glory do well at the ballot box. The situation will not be reversed by a mixture of electoral reforms and nostalgic speeches. We need a genuinely new approach to enable democracy to safeguard our future, or else thugs of various kinds will prevail.

I decided to write this book only recently and quite unexpectedly. I used to consider time and space as metaphysical categories with little relevance for practical politics. However, ruptures of time and space brought about by the Covid-19 pandemic made me read works written by colleagues from a variety of disciplines, showing that time and space are man-made and as such a subject of political engineering. I soon realized that our current political failures are not caused just by evil ideologies, greedy markets and inept leaders; they are also, if not primarily, a function of our poor handling of time and space. I was particularly influenced by a group of brilliant contemporary writers: Helga Nowotny, Saskia Sassen, Anne-Marie Slaughter, John Keane, Charles S. Maier and Wolfgang Merkel, to mention some of them. They made me curious about time and space, and confident about our capacity to get things right for the benefit of our planet and future generations. The process of bringing a book from its initial conception to publication is always pregnant with challenges. My special thanks go, therefore, to Joanna Godfrey and Emma Mateo, who have overseen each step of this book's production. I also wish to express my gratitude to friends who have commented on individual chapters: Stefania Bernini, Stephen E. Hanson, Martin Krygier, Wojciech Sadurski, Jacek Żakowski, Robert Zielonka and Radosław Zubek. I am equally indebted to the four anonymous reviewers recruited by Yale University Press.

Bruno Latour recently observed that the universal crisis that the Covid-19 lockdowns have exposed made us realize that we 'live with Earth, forever entangled, ensnared, enmired, overlapping, in and on top of each other, without being able to limit these ties to either cooperation or competition'.[2] The Russian invasion of Ukraine has also manifested the level of our enmeshment in time and space; the ghosts of history returned with a vengeance, and the fear of war and its price reached places far from Mariupol, Bucha and Kyiv. What can we do about this predicament? Can politics help us to cruise safely through the rapids of time and space? These are my major preoccupations in this book.

1

IN SEARCH OF THE LOST FUTURE

During the 2016 presidential campaign in the United States, I was shown a badge with the slogan 'Trump. America's Last Hope'. I found the slogan overly desperate in a country that prides itself on being the champion of the world. The promise of everlasting progress is the essence of the 'American dream', which means that if you currently experience some hardship there is no reason to worry because your children should, in any case, be better off than you. However, in 2017 the Pew Research Center established that only 37 per cent of Americans believe that today's children will grow up to be better off financially than their parents.[1] Americans were more optimistic than most Europeans, however. In France, only 9 per cent of those polled declared that their children would be better off, while a striking 71 per cent believed that they would be worse off. More than 60 per cent of Europeans declared in another study that they 'tend not to trust' their national government and parliament.[2] Asked how they would feel about reducing the number of national parliamentarians in their country and giving those seats to AI with access to their data, half of respondents, particularly the young, proved enthusiastic.[3] It looks as though some of us have lost faith in a democratic future – can the lost future be rescued and reclaimed?

You do not have to believe opinion polls to conclude that prospects for the future are hazy at best. The pandemic has killed millions and ruined the lives of many more 'supposedly fortunate' citizens, despite scientific advances and the heroic efforts of medical personnel. Despots such as Vladimir Putin have not been deterred from invading other states, killing innocent people and threatening a nuclear annihilation. Environmental degradation is progressing notwithstanding regular climate-change summits. Inequalities have reached unprecedented levels regardless of repeated pledges to reduce them.[4] Capitalism lurches from one crisis to another at the expense of ordinary families. We are now faced with cyber security threats on top of the better-known threats posed by nuclear weapons, tanks and machine guns in the hands of predatory states and fanatic individuals. None of this is fake news. We can argue about the gravity of this or that disaster, and question the prophets proclaiming the apocalypse.[5] We can point to *The Better Angels of Our Nature* or cite some cheerful economic statistics to make us less gloomy.[6] Yet it is hard to deny the accumulation of calamities for which we lack adequate responses. Young people are particularly scared.[7]

Of course, this is not the first time that the world seems to be on the brink, and yet we managed to bounce back. Think about the first half of the previous century torn by two devastating wars, Spanish flu, economic meltdown and fascism. But that cannot be a consolation; we must consider the victims of these past disasters and the price of getting us back to 'normal'. This is why I find ignoring and underplaying the seriousness of the current quandary either malicious or irresponsible. It is one thing to argue that the future is always uncertain and we are not necessarily on the 'way to hell'; another to assume that grave problems will somehow sort themselves out without major adjustments on our part.[8] As John Keane astutely put it: 'Humility in the face of new uncertainties – humans as wise shepherds rather than arrogant masters of the biosphere – is now mandatory. So is the re-imagining of democracy as a project of protecting humans and their biomes against ravages of power exercised arbitrarily.'[9]

Accelerated, unaccountable and unbalanced 'turbo-capitalism' is often blamed for depriving us of the future, but this book will focus on democratic politics as recommended by Keane.[10] After all, elected governments are supposed to protect us from external shocks such as financial meltdowns, foreign invasions, or epidemics.[11] They are mandated to keep the shortcomings of capitalism in check. They are entrusted to predict and avert environmental calamities, and mitigate the negative side-effects of technological advances. Governments should maintain order and make life predictable to some degree. Without this predictability, jobs and pensions are at

risk, while investments and even marriages become hazardous undertakings. Yet governments today are failing to perform these basic functions. They are simply administering the present with no plausible vision for the future. They rush from one crisis to another with no sense of direction. They prioritize their own territory although challenges facing them cannot be 'arrested' at any single border. Whilst elections can change the people in charge of a government, there is less and less hope that this turnover generates meaningful change, especially for the better. We seem to be ruled by WhatsApp government, to use Jonathan White's expression.[12] Many serious governmental deliberations and international negotiations are being conducted by speedy text messages full of bits and bytes with no records, agenda or underpinning vision.[13]

Populism and the personal flaws of our leaders are often seen as the reasons for the political disarray of today – but this book suggests a more fundamental explanation.[14] The future is increasingly grim because democratic politics is not suited for handling time and space in a way that safeguards the interests of future generations and overcomes state borders. To make the future meaningful and desirable we obviously need politicians with an ample time and space horizon, but even the most responsible statesmen are induced to take shortcuts because of the institutional set-up they find themselves hemmed in by. Democracy is currently tied to nation-states defending the selfish interests of a given territory and community. Democracy is also hostage to present-day voters with detrimental implications for future generations. This explains why politics stumbles in the ever more interdependent global environment, running at an ever faster pace. This explains why there is a growing feeling of democratic vulnerability and impotence despite all our technological advances. This explains why politics is increasingly out of sync with time and space.

Changing leaders or embracing new ideologies will not by itself resolve the kind of problems we are facing. We need to reform or even reinvent democracy and put in place a novel system of global governance.[15] Governance and democracy need to work in tandem; the former representing the 'output' of the political system, while the latter the 'input'.[16] Democracy can only thrive when supported by effective governance, and vice versa. Without strong governance, democracy will be unable to acquire a meaningful degree of control over time and space. Without strong democracy, governance becomes a bureaucratic device used by officials to make us comply with their arbitrary decisions. China is a telling example here.

I will argue that nation-states are not the only, let alone ideal, sites for either democracy or governance. However, both democracy and governance must envisage transparency, deliberation and citizens' involvement. I agree with Marc Plattner that it is hard to envisage good governance in the absence of democratic accountability, but there are various ways of assuring accountability, and national parliaments are often less effective in scrutinizing power holders than non-governmental organizations (NGOs) or the media.[17] This is why I propose to empower NGOs and professional associations. I also suggest spreading power between urban, national, regional and global units because each of them possesses different assets for handling time and space. States that we entrusted to manage time and space have proved poorly suited to perform this task in the internet era and they need help from local and transnational actors, formal and informal. The mode of democratic governance also needs to change. Governance can be less about adopting and enforcing rigid laws, and more about mediation, coordination and networking. We do not want to create a global empire of time and space, but rather to facilitate a democracy governing time and space for the benefit of the planet and its citizens.

Commanding time and space

In May 2020 the official newspaper of North Korea announced that the supreme leader, Kim Jong-un, is not really the master of time and space.[18] This came as a shock to millions of his citizens who were taught in schools that their supreme leader can magically fold time and cross space in a god-like manner. Suddenly they were told that this was a metaphor, and their great leader is only human, after all. His power was instantly diminished by this announcement, which prompted speculation about the future of his bizarre regime.

However, not only Kim Jong-un's fate is dependent on the ability to control time and space. Politicians and citizens in democratic states face a similar predicament. Time and space are precious treasures for all humans because we live through time and space, and both are scarce 'commodities'. We try to live longer, to move further and faster, and to improve the quality of our time and space. And yet, while we may dream about eternity and infinity, we fear that we only live in the here and now.[19]

Our time and space may well be limited, but we want to make the best of them. We go to schools, buy flats, or save for pensions to shape our future (sometimes trying to escape from our past). We move from place to place and communicate across different time zones and spaces to feel free and to live up to our full potential. We constantly remind ourselves that time should not be 'wasted': it is time for change, time to stop being complacent, time to turn the page. We tend to think that these are personal matters. In reality, they are largely determined by politics, which defines our (unequal) access to time and space according to dominant notions of justice, order and freedom. Those who control time and space have power, which explains why politics to a large extent has always been about these essential dimensions.

One of the ten commandments of the Old Testament is a telling example of chronopolitics: 'Six days you shall labour, and do all your work, but the seventh day is a Sabbath to the Lord your God.' (The term chronopolitics, coined by the American sociologist George W. Wallis, refers to the regulation, synchronization and allocation of time by politics.[20]) The Roman republican calendar, instituted around 509 BC, was a more comprehensive version of chronopolitics. The calendar was contested by different 'godly' rulers because calendar management was, to use Steve Henrix's words, about 'applying a man-made template over the movement of the Earth relative to the sun or the moon'.[21] When we celebrate our birthdays or renew our health insurance we do not realize that we are complying with the decrees of Pope Gregory XIII, who introduced a new calendar in the 1580s.

The politics of space have always been equally salient. As Charles S. Maier stated plainly on the cover of his epic work on space, power and borders: 'Throughout history, human societies have been organized pre-eminently as territories – politically bounded regions whose borders define the jurisdiction of laws and the movement of peoples.'[22] History books are chiefly about wars for territories. Walls have been raised and destroyed all over the globe. Our freedom of movement has always been conditioned by political decisions. When I was growing up in Communist Poland, we had no passport that would allow us to travel outside the country. Getting a passport often involved a bribe and readiness to spy on foreign friends. Getting the passport was only the first hurdle, as entering the 'free world' also required a visa, which was not straightforward either.

Political interventions in time and space are not necessarily crude, let alone violent. Governments of all modern states create financial incentives for women either to go to work or stay home and take care of children (a hot topic of exchange between feminists and paternalists). Students are encouraged to study either close to home, or overseas (a decision likely to influence not just their professional career, but also their worldview). Supermarkets are either kept closed or open on Sunday (a decision which shapes not only our private time-tables, but also our family or religious life).

Wake-up calls

We tend to realize the scale and scope of political interventions in time and space when confronted with external shocks such as wars or natural disasters. The first two months of Russia's full-scale invasion of Ukraine in 2022 'melted' the clocks that organized the lives of 40 million Ukrainians. In 1931, Salvador Dalí represented the fragility of time in his iconic painting *The Persistence of Memory*. Dalí's melted clock, draped over the dead limb of a tree, could well be placed on the ruins of Bucha or Mariupol to manifest that time does not always move forward in a solid, well-crafted, reassuring and predictable manner.

The Covid-19 pandemic could also be seen as an external shock reordering time and space. Lockdowns not only confined us to narrow spaces defined by the authorities; they also turned our future planning upside down and changed the implications of past decisions regarding our work and family life. Time has 'taken a break', and the meaning of space has

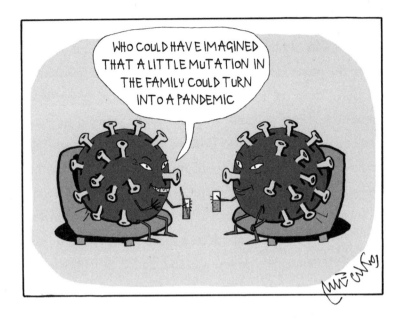

been changed by a series of decrees hastily adopted on the basis of conflicting and patchy evidence, and with little input from the confused and scared public.

The experience of this pandemic is important because epidemiologists believe that Covid-19 is now endemic in the human population, and it is not going to disappear any time soon. This means that some of the drastic measures intruding upon our time and space might remain or return, with uneven implications for different ages, genders, classes and ethnic and national groups. A common blueprint of restrictions imposed on citizens will vary because of different political cultures and the personal ambitions of leaders such as Modi, Erdoğan or Meloni. However, a common challenge in all countries will be to grasp the implications of individual political decisions, which affect the personal lives of citizens in uneven ways. Covid-prompted interventions in our time and space have not been guided by a quest for power, as was the case with the Russian invasion of Ukraine. However, they may well result in more power being concentrated in the hands of the executive with no sufficient democratic oversight, little genuine public deliberation, and shallow justification of the erratic measures reordering our time and space. As scholars have rightly pointed out, a series of grave financial, migratory, security and health shocks induced governments to rule by emergency decrees that de facto, if not de jure, suspended democratic procedures, and eroded civic liberties.[23]

Citizens need to address some fundamental questions. Which demands on my time are legitimate? Which restrictions on my movement am I prepared to tolerate? We are poorly equipped to answer these questions because our discussions about political choices have tended to move in a different direction. We used to argue about electoral preferences, the balance of power between state institutions, the rule of law and judicial independence. Although we talk about human and citizens' rights, these discussions focus chiefly on issues such as the freedom of speech or assembly, or the right to privacy or property. Our rights to control our use of time and space have been included in this discussion only indirectly, if ever. Economic discussions focused chiefly on the issues of competition, growth and redistribution. Some complained about foreign workers 'stealing our jobs', but even the most xenophobic politicians never advocated a total closure of national borders. Nevertheless, the pandemic has meant that policies that we previously found inconceivable, such as closing borders, have been introduced and legitimized. The scale of political intrusion into our time and space during the pandemic was unprecedented, at least in our own lifetimes. Although initially we found most of the drastic measures justified on medical grounds, slowly but surely, we began to realize how much we care about our freedom to move and utilize time freely. Now we know more than ever that our personal and collective life is lived through time and space.

Navigating in the fog

The impacts of the pandemic and war have made us recognize some simple truths about time and space, but we are not sure how to go about implementing them, especially in political terms. Some of us are more confident than I am about the way forward, but after five decades of studying politics, I know only one simple truth: there is nothing certain in the political world. This is not only because politics is about humans with different personalities, interests and skills. It is also, if not chiefly, because the context of politics is constantly on the move in response to changing technological, economic and social circumstances. Even conservatives appreciate the famous passage from *The Leopard* by Giuseppe Tomasi di Lampedusa: 'For things to remain the same, everything must change.'[24] But what exactly ought to change if we aspire to regain our grasp of the future?

Let me propose a special focus on nation-states and the way they handle time and space. Nation-states are the key political agents of security, welfare and peaceful change, even for those who treat the private sector as sacred. States control all major international organizations: the United Nations (UN), the International Monetary Fund (IMF), the World Health Organization (WHO), the European Union (EU) and the North Atlantic Treaty Organization (NATO). States are also the key sites for democratic accountability and representation. They define our rights and obligations, and it is their duty to use our money to make the world a better place. When states perform poorly, there is no hope and the future looks ugly.

Why are states, however resourceful and democratic, losing control over time and space? States are territorial organizations; they cannot function without borders. When borders begin to dissolve, states make no sense – and yet the past several decades have witnessed an incessant process of unbounding, a process during which the existing boundaries either wither, move or change nature. As I will show in a moment, some states were, and are still, trying to regain control over space, but with at best mixed results. This unbounding evolved in the field of geopolitics: think about the fall of the Soviet Union producing new states, autonomous enclaves, semi-protectorates and 'shared' neighbourhoods. Unbounding then accelerated in the field of economics: globalization and the EU single market are the most cited examples. In a world of increased connectivity, unbounding has also progressed in

14

the field of health: Covid-19, HIV/AIDS and antibiotic resistance have spread across borders with remarkable ease. Unbounding has also exploded in the field of communication, with the internet reaching even the most remote places within three short decades. Territorial states are increasingly helpless in handling transnational flows of money, goods, people, messages and viruses. Yet we lack a viable transnational public authority. The United Nations and even the European Union are toothless – partly because nation-states are reluctant to delegate meaningful powers and resources to them.

Nation-states also suffer from short-sightedness. When states look backward, they only see past glories, when they look forward, they see almost nothing. States have repeatedly failed to predict and avert natural calamities. Their record of creating disasters such as war or economic anarchy is also notable. Unfortunately, democracy is partly responsible for states' short-termism. Democracy requires regular rotations of the government. That not only limits these governments' time perspectives, but also binds them to the wishes of the electorate of the day, and prompts the neglect of future generations. As Andreas Schäfer and Wolfgang Merkel put it bluntly in the *Oxford Handbook of Time and Politics*: 'Since democracies are "systematically biased in favor of the present", they tend to neglect the future and impair the rights of future sovereigns.'[25] And Jonathan Boston added: 'There is a widespread belief, based on multiple forms of empirical evidence, that democratically elected governments, when

faced with intertemporal conflicts, display a tendency to favour short-term interests over long-term interests.'[26] No wonder numerous young people are giving up on democracy.[27] They are likely to work longer for less money than their parents in a degraded natural environment.[28]

What kind of future?

Political failure to secure the future has generated calls for reinforcing states at the expense of globalization and democracy. Borders, and walls, are again in vogue and so is the resurgence of territorial power politics backed by military force. In February 2022, President Putin declared that his invasion of Ukraine is to secure Russia's future. Autocratic China prides itself on being a strong state able to secure the future of its citizens better than the democratic world. Softer versions of sovereigntism calling for the primacy of the nation-state, governed according to the principle of national sovereignty, over local and supranational governance structures, are also popular in Europe.[29] Brexit proved more about taking back control over borders than about bringing power back from Brussels to Westminster. In Hungary and Poland democracy was sacrificed on the altar of nativist ambitions. Sovereigntism, as a distorted form of nationalism, is also in vogue in the Middle East and Asia-Pacific. The 'America first' policy of President Trump, advocating walls against migrants and barriers to international trade, was part of this trend to turn the clock back: nation-states must be rebuilt and international cooperation rolled back. Democracy, according to some, could also be sacrificed in order for the leader to stay at the helm. We saw this on 6 January 2021, when supporters of President Trump attacked the Capitol Building in Washington, DC.

I find this sovereigntist vision of the future misguided and dangerous. This is not because I dismiss the significance of military might, ridicule national identity, or cheer the demise of states. I simply believe that we should not, willy-nilly, accept a world in which those with money and weapons can ignore laws and moral norms. In other words, we should strive for the rules-based world order envisaged by Grotius and Kant and not reconcile ourselves with the chaotic and conflict-ridden world described by Machiavelli and Hobbes.[30] It matters what kind of future we embrace. Do we want to preserve or destroy our planet? Do we believe in the rule of law or the rule of force? Is the future an option only for some 'chosen' nations, classes or ethnic groups?

The sovereigntist conception of the future can also be challenged on empirical grounds. Control over borders and territory is still being claimed all over the world.[31] The question is whether these claims do any good to our planet and respective citizens. Has Putin's invasion of Ukraine made Russians more secure and prosperous? Will annexation of Taiwan make Chinese people more resourceful and respected? Technological know-how together with the skills and motivation of the workforce are today the most crucial assets, none of which are obtainable by territorial gains, especially those involving conquest by force. Security is also enhanced better by human development and economic sustainability than by a military build-up alone. Why are neighbours of Russia so determined to be part of the EU, which does not have any army?

China has certainly been successful in generating technological innovation and economic growth, but it has been less successful in coping with an ageing population, environmental degradation and foreign debt.[32] If the time horizon of China's rulers is indeed longer than that displayed by democracies, why does China emit more carbon dioxide than any other state in the world? If Russia knows how to secure the future of its citizens, why is the life expectancy of Russians lower than for the citizens of Morocco, Honduras or Sri Lanka?

States are not withering away, nor are borders becoming meaningless. However, states need more intelligence, flexibility and purpose, not muscle. If they want to get things done, they need to abandon the pretence of being the 'only game in town', and become smarter through collaboration with NGOs, city authorities, international organizations and transnational markets. Shared power is more effective than sovereign power, as shown in the 'war' against the pandemic. Vaccine nationalism and international travel bans proved to be inadequate responses to a virus that does not recognize state borders, and whose spread required differentiated responses by different territorial units operating within different time horizons. Emergency medical assistance and civil protection were most skilfully handled by regional and urban units, while economic recovery schemes could only be secured by transnational institutions such as the EU.[33] States which accepted power-sharing principles early on, and engaged in networking with other centres of authority, coped with the virus much better than those running their response heavy-handedly from national capitals ignoring local and international factors. The pandemic was yet another confirmation that national sovereignty is easier to declare than to achieve in practice. In the contemporary world, states can only punch their weight when working in concert with other actors – which explains why I endorse networks and networking.

I do not expect China or Russia to take the lead in pushing for the changes recommended here, but I hope that liberal democracies will lead by example in making the future meaningful and something to be treasured. Democracies must regain their sex appeal by showing that they are able to diffuse territorial conflicts, halt climate change and generate welfare for future generations. In essence, they need to manifest novel ways of mastering time and space. This is key to winning the competition with the despotic world.[34]

Yet before stating what the *new* politics of time and space should imply, we need to examine the *old* politics and understand what went wrong. Since space and time are intricate if not mysterious assets, we need to establish their political meanings. We also need to reflect on the spatial and temporal dimensions of the world that has passed, because it has numerous practical implications for our lives as individuals and collectives. This is what this book is about. It tells us how politics has been shaping space and time across history for a variety of good and bad reasons, with uneven implications for citizens. From history, we will move to tomorrow and try to envisage a new cosmopolis: a world resembling a multicultural global city inhabited by people who respect each other and try to save the planet. It's time to regain control over our space and reclaim our future. For the future is not merely imagined, it is also made.

2

ORDERING TIME

Why does China, which extends across 4,893 kilometres, have only one time zone? Why has Lithuania switched time zones five times throughout the 1990s and early 2000s? Why has the European Union decided to abandon the obligatory one-hour clock change in summer and winter? In all these cases, the rationale was political. China used to have five time zones, but imposing only one across this vast country helped the Communist government to assert centralized control over its diverse and geographically dispersed people. (In defiance of the central government, the Uyghurs in the far-western Xinjiang province continue to covertly use their own 'Xinjiang Time'.) After the fall of the Soviet Union, politicians in Lithuania could not make up their minds whether their time zone should reflect lingering ties with Russia or prospective links with Western Europe. The European Commission responded to growing Euroscepticism by proposing to abandon its summer/winter time directive in 2019. As the Commission President Jean-Claude Juncker put it, 'There is no applause when EU law dictates that Europeans have to change the clocks twice a year.'[1]

Calendars represent another time-framing device used by politicians to challenge existing notions of what is natural, rational and good. The specific objectives may vary, but some politicians are convinced that calendars help them to acquire and legitimize new powers. Julius Caesar decided to consolidate reforms across his vast empire by replacing the multitude of inaccurate and diverse calendars of the Roman commonwealth with a single official one carrying the emperor's name. Robespierre in Revolutionary France changed the seven-day week into a decimal week to desacralize the cycle of work and rest. Stalin attempted to institute a five-day week in the Soviet Union and, in order to break traditional patterns of socialization among families, the rest day was randomly assigned by the authorities. Mustafa Kemal Atatürk abandoned the Muslim calendar in Turkey to push ahead the separation of state and church. Pol Pot declared 'Year Zero' in Cambodia to break with all forms of power that preceded him.

However, the framing of time can also assume less formalized guises – with equally serious implications. According to Christopher McIntosh, President Trump attempted to create and maintain 'an indefinite present' by discounting the past and future of American politics and pronouncing the glorious present exemplified by his own rule.[2] Trump seemed to believe that anything other than his own leadership would signify the end of history and the end of efforts to Make America Great Again. This may have been one of the reasons underpinning his refusal to accept the 2020 election results.

Time framing may well be abused by power holders, but it fulfils important functions. Time allocations and regulations allow people to go through their lives with a reassuring degree of order, stability, rhythm and structure. Time measures delineate past and future, regress and progress, birth and death, transience and permanence. Citizens need to know how time flows in order to adjust their personal planning accordingly. Calendars, time zones and the clock-defined job schedule help citizens to make 'rational' choices regarding their family, money, work and education. The ordering of time installs predictability and gives citizens a sense of security. Citizens want to know at least roughly what the future will bring, and they want to sense the expected timeframes of future events: will they be cyclical or linear, short or long, repetitive or cumulative, slow or fast, measured or experienced? They want to compare the timeframes in their country with those of other countries. (Jenny Shaw has analysed the popular belief that, in different parts of the world and in different kinds of places, life proceeds at different speeds.)[3]

Citizens can try to press the government for a different direction and speed of future development, but in a world deprived of a sense of time structure, destructive chaos prevails. As globalization, climate change and technological innovation impose new timeframes, citizens' insecurity only grows. Calendars, time

23

zones, working hours and other forms of regulation, synchronization and allocation of time can inject a sense of stability if not security.

However, these time-framing devices work better in periods of stability than turmoil. If the present is perceived as a crisis, governments are unable to lay solid foundations for tomorrow. Uncertainty, fear, and subsequently chaos, begin to dominate political decision-making, with implications for ordinary citizens. We have experienced this phenomenon first-hand during the recent health and financial crises. Instead of reassuring citizens and instilling a sense of hope for the future, the authorities, perhaps unwittingly, made people despair. This state of affairs was more evident in Trump's America or Modi's India than in Merkel's Germany, for instance – which only suggests that policies based on scientific evidence can install a sense of predictability and confidence better than those based on post-truth.

Russia's invasion of Ukraine has also generated policies that have unsettled citizens, especially in Europe. Citizens in countries bordering Ukraine, Belarus and Russia have obviously been more exposed to Russia's brutal behaviour than citizens in the rest of Europe. Yet long-term planning became difficult also in the south of Europe, Africa and Asia, especially as a consequence of energy and food dependency on Ukrainian and Russian exports. The war has also highlighted discrepancies in time-frames. Desperate Ukrainians had a long wait for the EU to decide on and deliver aid to their besieged country. How many lives could have been saved if the EU decision-making process was less protracted? As for those who fled Ukraine, time became a long waiting process with no clear end in sight. I will never forget the many Ukrainian women wandering with their children through the parks of Warsaw; I suspect with many hopes but few plans for the future. Different timeframes could also be observed in Ukraine itself. While ordinary citizens were forced to focus on everyday survival, the policy-makers were considering the long-term implications of their successive moves, as a way of assuring that Ukraine does indeed have a future. But before we consider the uses and misuses of time framing by politicians, let us reflect on the nature of time. This has implications for our understanding of the politics of time.

Is time real?

We often think about time as we think about the air that we inhale. It is something that we take for granted, given by God or nature to all humans on this Earth. Politics hardly enters our considerations here; time just keeps rolling regardless of who is in charge of governments.

Yes, we know that the timespan of our own life is difficult to predict but we assume that a single day has 24 hours, and a year has 365 days. Time and its 'organic' structure helps us to move forward within the labyrinth of complex modern society. Moreover, time seems to guide our life by giving it identity and meaning. Time tells us where we come from – the past, where we have been; the present, where we currently are; the

future, where we are headed towards. Time tells us what we can or cannot aspire to, because many ambitions cannot be reached in our lifetime, while other desires are superseded by the flow of time. Time inspires us and disciplines us at the same time. Without time we may be lost in the universe, deprived of footpaths and signposts. A politician who intends to deprive us of a natural, steady and predictable flow of time would not be able to count on our vote, would they?

However, the reality of life is often different than it seems. Physicists tell us that the structure of time is not as uniform, universal, measurable or predictable as we tend to assume. For instance, time passes more quickly on the top of a mountain than down in the valley. The lower you are, the slower time passes. Time also runs more slowly for objects or people moving at high speed. These findings are not just theoretical; they have been experimentally confirmed, even though our simple watches do not grasp these differences. If time is not uniform, to use Carlo Rovelli's words, it has a 'different rhythm in every different place', and 'passes here differently from there'.[4] Rovelli and most other physicists echo Albert Einstein who proved that time is relative, not absolute, as Isaac Newton had claimed a few centuries earlier. Einstein questioned the distinction between the past, present and future not just in theoretical physics, but also in the trajectories of individual lives. When his friend Michele Besso died, Einstein wrote to his family that although Michele had preceded him in death it was of no consequence, because 'for us physicists the separation between past, present, and future is only an illusion, although a convincing one'.[5]

Moreover, if the difference between past and future does not exist, neither does the difference 'between cause and effect, between memory and hope, between regret and intention', Rovelli concluded in a philosophical manner.[6] A decade ago, the British physicist Julian Barbour went further and declared boldly that time does not exist at all, and that the concept of time has therefore no place in physics.[7] This won him the first prize in a prestigious essay competition in contemporary cosmology, organized by the celebrated Foundational Questions Institute (FQXi). Barbour's simple reasoning could appeal to a broader public: 'I believe in a timeless universe for the childlike reason that time cannot be seen – the emperor has no clothes.'[8]

Does politics enter these cosmological considerations? Yes, of course. If time is not given by God or nature, then it is clearly a human invention and, as such, subject to political engineering. If time is not linear or uniform, then the question is: who decides about time structure, and why? There is no need to assume sinister motivations on the part of politicians. Time may well be only an illusion, but it performs numerous useful functions for our societies. However, most political decisions generate winners and losers. Not all decisions generate the promised results. And there are always procedural questions: do those deciding about our time have the mandate to do so? I will return to these questions later, but first let me mention another political consideration stemming from Einstein's legacy. It has to do with our ambition to shape the future.

If we can overcome the barrier of time, we can achieve things previously unthinkable. Newton's belief in eternal laws and time suggests political fatalism, while Einstein's general theory of relativity, which allows for the possibility of time travel both to the future and the past, justifies political optimism and idealism. Rovelli went even further and suggested that a life without time is more beautiful and full of opportunities than one with time.[9] We can even move to another planet in search of a better future. The latter is a recurrent motif of many science-fiction books and movies. *Interstellar*, the 2014 epic directed and produced by Christopher Nolan, envisaged an escape from the dying Earth in search of a new home for mankind by defying our understanding of time. In a memorable scene starring Michael Caine and Jessica Chastain, the high-ranking NASA scientist is told by his younger colleague: 'You are afraid of time. For years you have been trying to change equations without changing the underlying assumptions about time . . . It's nonsensical.' (Kip Thorne, a theoretical physicist and Nobel Prize Laureate, served as scientific consultant to this movie.)

It should be mentioned that a small group of physicists, Lee Smolin most prominent among them, maintain that 'our experience of the world, our perception of change, our feeling of being in the present, and all other human perceptions related to temporality, are not mere illusions'.[10] Time is real, according to Smolin, but this does not necessitate a fatalistic worldview. Smolin concedes that in his model 'there is no going back and adjusting the past', but insists that we can still 'choose the future'.[11] In his view, humans have the power to exert control over climate change, economic systems and technology because time is real rather than illusory.

The making of time

Whether time is real or illusory is not, however, the key political concern. In the world of politics, the crucial question is: who makes time, and how? Helga Nowotny, a prominent European intellectual, gives a straightforward answer to this question: 'Time is made by human beings and has to do with power which they exercise over one another with the aid of strategies of time.'[12] While it is true that time cannot be seen, heard, smelled or tasted, our daily experience bears witness to the fact that time is variously being measured, imposed, shortened, suspended and anticipated. Time is controlled, abstracted, objectified, bought and sold, made and reshaped. Human beings do all that, albeit with reference to gods, nature and science. 'In a world without people,' adds another famous thinker, Norbert Elias, 'there would be no time. There would be no clocks and no calendars.'[13]

Time is a powerful political instrument because our life is dependent on it and the ways in which it is regulated by governments. Regulations tell us when we should begin education, pay debts, work or rest. They specify the age we are allowed to have sex, wed, vote, or retire from work. They tell us when elections should be held, what the time limit is to prosecute crimes, the duration within which we can return a defective product, and how long someone can hold public office.

In democracies, laws are supposed to be made with the consent of citizens, but time is often presented as something natural, and as such beyond the usual processes of political bargaining. In the tribal rituals described by Norbert Elias, the making of time takes place behind masks, suggesting that time is created by gods and demons. Priests have been in the position of setting and controlling time for a large part of human history, and were only replaced by scientists with the rise of natural science in the seventeenth century, usually identified with Galileo, the Tuscan 'father' of modern physics. Isaac Newton, who formulated the laws on motion and universal gravitation a century later, led us to believe that time exists objectively as a part of natural creation. Yet social scientists such as Durkheim, Weber, Marx, Elias and Castells saw time as an instrument of social engineering, helping people to orient themselves in the complex environment surrounding them and to create (or maintain) hierarchies of power. This approach does not necessarily view time as subjective, but it underlines the point that time is primarily made by and for humans.

Why do some of those in charge of time framing try to conceal their involvement? Perhaps this is because time is allocated utterly unfairly to different members of society, and hence it is convenient for those framing time to create the impression that time is something natural rather than man-made. Helga Nowotny talks about the different rhythms for diverse classes, genders and regions. Those who are privileged go through life at high speed, while the unemployed and dispossessed often feel that time has come to a standstill. Women more than men are under pressure to 'invest' their time in their home and caring duties. Time has a different meaning, price and pace in the countryside and in mega-cities. The more complex the society, the more diversified the sequences of time, and the more blurred the hierarchies of power. Barbara Adam constructed a tree of temporal hierarchies that features such dichotomies as trade over giving, commodity over caring, speed over a slow process, public time over private time, financial wealth over time wealth, objective economic time and subjective lived time, and so on.[14] Most of these hierarchies of power emerged gradually without bearing the 'finger prints' of a particular ruler. The agency behind time framing is therefore difficult to trace, even though the history books often focus on individual time-framers such as Julius Caesar, Josef Stalin or Mustafa Kemal Atatürk.

The mode of time framing has evolved tremendously throughout the ages, depending on technological innovations and societal trends. It took several thousand years for people to learn how to produce calendars which were able to organize time more precisely than reliance on the movement of the moon and the sun. The first public clock was installed on the tower of Palazzo Vecchio in Florence in the early fourteenth century, and five centuries later public clocks were on display in town squares and factories across the entire world, mobilizing and disciplining citizens. The most famous amongst them, such as London's Big Ben, completed in 1859, or the City Hall Clock in Philadelphia, installed in 1894, have been vivid symbols of the authority public time holds. The internet transformed these eminent clocks into mere tourist attractions, however.[15] Network time has replaced clock time. As Robert Hassan explains: 'Network time constitutes a new and powerful temporality that is beginning to displace, neutralise, sublimate and otherwise upset other temporal relationships in our work, home and leisure environment.'[16] A new type of society, a network society, was born with the explosion of digital communication. The internet made real-time exchanges possible, irrespective of geographic distances and administrative borders. It has compressed time unlike any previous technology, and in effect created synchronic individuals who live only in the present, disconnected from both past and future.[17] This observation may not apply equally to all social groups, but it is hard to deny that the internet has changed us beyond recognition.

Public time

Time was always a collective endeavour because it helps individuals to relate to each other. It offers us a familiar collective frame for acting, and a common benchmark to measure our achievements. Yet the notion of public time emerged only two or three centuries ago, chiefly to describe time as subject to government regulations and, hopefully, building trust, fostering a sense of community, encouraging solidarity, but also imposing order and discipline.[18] Social scientists point to technological innovations and the Industrial Revolution as factors behind the central framing of time, but students of politics cannot but remark that the formation of the nation-state coincides with the notion of public time. The eminent American historian, Charles S. Maier studied the writings on time by Thomas Hobbes and John Locke and concluded: 'For Hobbes, war, and for Locke, wealth, required establishment of the state; and neither war nor wealth could be specified without a concept of continuity across time.'[19] States could create expectations that security and welfare will persist through time and not fall victim to ever-changing and fragile medieval governance arrangements. Adopting a linear and smooth conception of time with the help of clocks and calendars was seen as a symbol of rational order: a 'triumph of diligence over decay'.[20]

Consolidating the bounded territory of nascent states also required the standardization and homogenization of time. It did not make sense to have different times in New York and Philadelphia or London and Reading, especially since trains started to commute between nearby cities. Linear, standardized public time also became a source of social mobilization that newly created states could rely on for economic and security reasons. Universal citizenship in nation-states went hand in hand with universal (male) conscription – an obligation for a fixed and predictable period of time. Gradually states imposed their schedules on citizens in numerous other fields, especially in the field of work, transport and commerce. This could not but stir up some (albeit futile) resistance. Some accused governments in charge of time reforms of playing God, others of exploiting workers' labour. Ian P. Beacock cites a grumpy British reader writing to the *Spectator* in 1907 that time reform 'proposes to put us to bed and get us up by

Act of Parliament. Personally, I like to choose my own time for these operations.'[21]

In the end, governments have managed to get their way in regulating time, although with some national variations. France adopted a nationwide mean time in 1891 but refused to adopt the Greenwich meridian, which was seen as too English for them. This leads to another important observation, namely that time reforms played a crucial role in building and consolidating the nation in nascent states. A good illustration is provided by Thomas M. Allen's book on the early years of the United States of America, suggestively titled *A Republic in Time*.[22] Modern nationalism required the invention of a 'stable and, crucially, empty temporal container within which national affiliation can express itself'.[23] Clock time helped the fathers of the American nation-state to overcome modes of temporal experience based in religion, nature and dynastic hierarchies. The rational, standardized and value-free temporal structures proved central to modern nationhood, and not just to industrial and commercial development as is often argued. Allen points to the narratives of such well-known nineteenth-century writers as Catharine Beecher, Henry Thoreau and Ralph Waldo Emerson who painted America as a 'nation in time'.[24]

According to Oliver Zimmer, the motto 'one clock fits all' was also central to the formation of the German nation and a unified German state.[25] Speaking before the Reichstag in 1891, General von Moltke argued for merging Germany's five time zones into one, using powerful nationalist and statist rhetoric. For the most acclaimed German soldier, all strong and powerful nations must become tightly integrated states and a single time standard is a way to meet this objective. 'Since we have become an empire, it is only right and proper,' argued Moltke, 'to do away with multiple time zones.'[26] Local authorities adopted even more nationalistic and somewhat Romantic language on the eve of the time unification, even though it represented a serious challenge to long-standing residential habits and customs. Zimmer quotes a local newspaper arguing with joy that when all clocks would be in 'complete agreement', the whole of Germany would shout their festive greetings at the stroke of midnight: 'For the glowing patriot, this commonality in festive spirit is very pleasant to say the least.'[27]

Time played a similar role in the early Republican era in Turkey. For President Atatürk, the standardization and secularization of time was a means of creating not just a well-functioning state, but also modern citizens. According to Mehmet Kendirci, time was employed as 'an instrument to represent political power and to legitimate the early Republican governing elite'.[28] Kendirci cites Atatürk's famous speech in 1925 where he outlined his vision of linking modernity with daily life practices based on the values of their age. In the opinion of the founding father of the Republic of Turkey, sheiks, dervishes and disciples should not dictate religious schedules to enlightened Turkish citizens. A single clock time and secular calendar should therefore superimpose religious ones.

Technology, ideology and power

Most scholars of time emphasize the role of technology in underpinning the change of public perceptions on time. In a widely discussed book, *The Culture of Time and Space, 1880–1918*, Stephen Kern argued that technological innovations cutting across distance and timespans – the telephone, wireless telegraph, x-ray, radio, cinema, automobile and airplane – altered dimensions of life and thought. Existing social systems where everything has 'its time and place' began to look illusory and outdated. The distinction between the past, the present and the future appeared ever more blurred. New cultural hierarchies, administrative systems and economic modes of growth could therefore emerge. Other scholars emphasized the role of clocks and watches. Alexis McCrossen argued that public clocks were key symbols of strong governments and national identity.[29] McCrossen is seconded by Randall Stevenson, who illustrated how politicians sought to impose the clock's rule over people's lives by introducing daylight saving time and pub closing hours.[30] As synchronizing time and keeping time discipline became a symbol of modern citizenship, people started to treat access to time as their natural right. Possession of clocks and watches became widespread, augmenting the influence of not only clock- and watchmakers, but also of the regulating authorities. In Germany, according to Oliver Zimmer, the railway rather than the clock was the prime driver of time perceptions. The railways were portrayed as time machines, acting as 'large national clocks'.[31] Clearly the huge impact of new technologies has been experienced before the invention of the internet and artificial intelligence, and contemporary students of the internet must be experiencing a feeling of déjà vu.

Yet technology, however important, was (and still is) a mere instrument of altering the existing hierarchies of power and institutional arrangements. Synchronized time made it easier for governments to assert control and discipline within nascent nation-states. The assertion of public time, as opposed to the organic or private one, was a crucial political device to make people comply with official orders. Technology to measure and standardize time has stimulated economic growth and made public institutions work more rationally. However, it also helped these public institutions to curb civil liberties, and the rights of workers. No wonder the new notion of time had begun to be questioned by such leading novelists as Oscar Wilde, Joseph Conrad, Marcel Proust, Franz Kafka and James Joyce.[32] Proust found the official public time superficial, Kafka terrifying, and Joyce arbitrary. Joseph Conrad articulated an even more vivid reaction against coordinated universal standardizations of time exemplified by Greenwich Mean Time (GMT). In his 1907 book, *The Secret Agent*, a Russian anarchist attempts to blow up the symbol of centralized political authority: the Greenwich Observatory. (Conrad's plot is based on the true story of the so-called Greenwich Bombing of 1894 by the French anarchist Martial Bourdin.)

Novelists were supported by academics such as Émile Durkheim, who juxtaposed the rhythm of private and public spheres of life.[33] Both writers and scholars started to distinguish between internally experienced time, and external time as imposed by the government. They distanced themselves from the uniform, homogenous and universal notion of time and argued that individuals create many different times through their individual lifestyles.[34] Time for them was chiefly subjective, relative, reversible, intermittent and heterogeneous.

The rise of Fascist and Communist regimes vindicated suspicions about the uses and misuses of public time. Since time 'took on the character of a plastic medium by the very process of being measured, equipartitioned, and packaged' there was a growing temptation to make it subject to the capricious political will of the government of the day.[35] And so the Nazi and Communist parties tried to expropriate time from individuals to make the entirety of time available for the state and its objectives. Soviet officials at different levels of administration had to adjust to Stalin's habit of working at night, because missing a phone call from the leader could have grave implications for them. It is said that a light was always on in the Kremlin to make it look like Stalin was always working. The work time of ordinary citizens was shaped not by the market but by the state apparatus and the ruling party. Personal time was also 'nationalized' as families were asked to conduct life according to instructions coming from the state. Holidays spent in state-run resorts with families of fellow labourers became a proud symbol of Communism and Fascism. As Stephen Hanson observed, 'The goal of Soviet socialism was to organize production in such a manner as to master time itself . . . if work was done intensively enough, according to the party's direction, time could actually be compressed, and the conflict between labour and leisure ultimately overcome.'[36] This proved to be an illusion, as has the Fascist claim that time can be frozen so that the 'glorious Nazi rule' can last for ever.[37]

Time in democracy

The defeat of Fascism and the spread of democracy in a large part of the world reinstated private time and did away with totalitarian notions of public time. Nation-states have persisted, however, overseeing huge bureaucracies eager to regulate time for the 'benefit' of citizens. Some of these regulations relate to technical matters. Maritime, road and air traffic, television broadcasting or the use of digital space require detailed schedules, synchronization, and time slots. These regulations make our life easier, but they are not necessarily benign and non-partisan. Air traffic or broadcasting regulations benefit some commercial or political actors more than others; they also have environmental or security implications. The more technology enters our private lives, the more public regulation is required, in turn affecting our personal lives. For instance, those of us who will have access to the fifth generation of cellular technology, 5G, will be able to enjoy much greater speed for wireless devices than those without 5G – but

we will also be more exposed to privacy breaches. Additional problems stem from our growing dependence on these regulations. Inadequate regulation is often better than no regulation whatsoever, as we experienced after the rise of digital social media, such as Facebook.

Regulating the time of work and commercial activity also has a profound impact on our lives, and I will talk about this in depth later. However, the most sensitive political questions are raised by time-related regulations dealing with citizenship, judiciary and democratic representation. The law determines how old we need to be to acquire the right to vote, how long elected officials can hold office, and the length of electoral cycles. Governments decide when resident aliens can apply for naturalization and how long they need to wait for a decision.

41

Citizens are asked to pay tax on a certain date. Convicted criminals are punished with prison sentences of varying durations. Abortion is only allowed in a restricted timeframe. Social welfare benefits can be claimed according to a timetable defined by the government.

All public institutions confront citizens with numerous schedules and deadlines. Some deal with permissions, others with benefits, yet others with duties. There is hardly any administrative matter that does not envisage time-related arrangements. We understand that all these laws and regulations are supposed to make the life of public institutions orderly and reliable. But even so, one may query whether it is fair to deprive people of certain benefits simply because they missed a government-imposed deadline?

Elizabeth F. Cohen from Syracuse University tried to address these queries in the American context and she concluded that the existing laws and procedures devaluate some people's political time and this, according to her, constitutes a widely overlooked form of injustice. In her 2018 book entitled *The Political Value of Time*, Cohen examines various forms of 'temporal boundaries', which deny rights to certain groups of people that other groups usually enjoy. She points to racialized incarceration, hindered naturalization, differentiated visa systems and obstructionist abortion waiting periods to demonstrate widespread 'temporal injustices'.[38] Although time is not usually conceived of as a 'good' granted and managed by states, her study shows that it should, in fact, be treated like a precious object. Time is something that people badly need, and it therefore represents a democratic good, according to Cohen. Moreover, time's political value is based on 'beliefs about durational time's role in a set of processes that are themselves integral to democratic politics'.[39] Official schedules, deadlines, moments and dates are used by states to 'transact over power'. Deadlines of all sorts impose boundaries on citizens' choices and opportunities, while schedules impose uneven burdens on different groups of citizens.

If time is used in an unjust manner, why do citizens not rebel? Why are time-related regulations hardly ever an object of political bargaining, if not conflict? One possible answer would suggest that the unfair distribution of time affects 'weak' groups of citizens such as incarcerated criminals. More often than not, non-citizens, first-generation immigrants or migrants, are treated unfairly by governmental deadlines and schedules. These groups, disproportionally affected by unfair regulations, have limited bargaining power. However, Cohen offers other plausible explanations. Time is experienced by citizens in a way that gives it a guise of universality and scientific neutrality. Clock and calendar time, in particular, appear to be more egalitarian and less partial than other traditional means of making political claims. The clock ticks and calendar days pass at the same rate, regardless of someone's social class, status or birth. When devices rather than humans appear to control and measure time, we do not suspect them of prejudice. Quantified time seems to be freed from subjective, irrational intrusion. Decision-making based on scientifically measured time seems therefore rational, fair and non-biased. It is worth recalling the tribal ritual of making time behind masks, described by Norbert Elias. In democracy, however, the 'masks' are not righteous gods or demons, but science.

Time is power

Christopher Clark, an Australian historian based in Cambridge, opens his book *Time and Power: Visions of History in German Politics, from the Thirty Years' War to the Third Reich* with the following sentence: 'As gravity bends light, so power bends time.'[40] Yet this dictum can easily be reversed. Politicians bend time because time gives them enormous power. This rule has persisted over ages. David S. Landes, who studied time making in eighth- to twelfth-century T'ang and Sung China, established that in this context, the calendar was a symbol of sovereignty: each emperor inaugurated his reign with the promulgation of his calendar, and his astronomers had the monopoly on using timekeeping instruments. This is because emperors understood that 'Knowledge of the right time and season was power, for it was this knowledge that governed both the acts of everyday life and decisions of state.'[41] Today the machinery of government is more complex, and many governments are subject to democratic oversight. Nevertheless, governments try to keep time outside the usual processes of political contestation, as if time were a matter of science rather than power. The more sophisticated the technology we use, the more we are dependent on time, and power ends up in the hands of governments as a result. State and inter-state institutions are also becoming ever more complex, and hence have a greater need for schedules and deadlines beyond the control of citizens. However, we lack the narrative to talk about time in terms of power. Time hardly ever features in handbooks of political science, even though politics is chiefly about power.[42] Why time is seldom discussed by parliaments is also a mystery to me.

How can we ensure that decisions regarding time are democratic? The first step would be to acknowledge that time is not absolute, but relative. In fact, there are multiple notions of time, most of them hybrid, and a proper or truthful notion of time does not exist. Admitting that time is made by us humans is the required second step. Time is socially constructed to serve numerous individual and collective aims, power being the most prominent among them. The link between the state and time should be appreciated and informed by the evolving technological and ideological trends. The next step would be to map 'temporal injustices' in our own distinct states. In states such as Italy the statute of judicial limitation is a thorny topic because it allows tax evaders to escape justice. In states such as Poland the most problematic issue is likely to be the limited timeframe for abortion. The final step would be for citizens to raise their voices and demand justice in the politics of time framing. Justice cannot be done without citizens' participation. Time, like any other democratic good, should be made 'by' citizens, and not merely 'for' citizens by their respective governments, however enlightened. When will this happen? I do not know, but I am happy to trust the optimistic view of Ryszard Kapuściński, a Polish novelist, who once observed: 'Somewhere in the world circulates mysterious energy which will approach and fill us up with strength to unlock time – action will then begin.'[43]

3

NOMADS AND SETTLERS

One of the most popular songs in the late 1970s was 'Father and Son' by Cat Stevens, and it nicely grasped a contrast between nomads and settlers. The father urged the son to settle down, because this is what had made him happy. The son's answer, however, was a flat refusal, because he yearned to leave. The song was about change, not space, and about different lifestyles, not about different perceptions of territory. Yet nomads and settlers always treat territory in a different manner. Settlers are fond of fences and walls because they provide them with a sense of property, stability and community. Nomads traverse fences and walls in search of a better life, new friends or adventure. Even very different groups of nomads, such as refugees and frequent-flyer globetrotters, have one fundamental thing in common: for them space is to be traversed, and borders to be crossed. In contrast, open-ended space is treated by settlers as a threat, and not as an opportunity. Freedom of movement represents a basic human right for nomads, but settlers do their best to restrict freedom of movement through visa systems, trade quotas or cultural othering.[1]

Our approach to space and the freedom of movement has never been simple.[2] Early settlers and ranchers were fond of raising walls and fences, while hunters, migrants and wanderers argued against them. Children, women and people without 'proper' documentation still have their freedom of movement constrained by law within some countries. Homeless people are forbidden to sleep rough on the streets of some cities. There are heated discussions about the margin of movement appropriate for different kinds of detainees. In war zones and in some undemocratic states, ethnic groups are being evicted from their settlements and forced to migrate. But, as Saskia Sassen has documented, expulsions from professional livelihood, from living space, even from the very biosphere that makes life possible, are now common even in wealthy democracies.[3]

Unbounding and re-bounding are equally pronounced and contested in the international context. The trans-border movement of goods, capital, services and labour has been praised by some and scorned by others in different times and places. Migrants have been seen either as a threat or as an opportunity in both cultural and economic terms. The free circulation of ideas was feared by despots, traditionalists and devotees, but it was welcomed by artists and rebels. Liberals have always argued that open borders generate knowledge and profits. Some even claim that cross-border trade generates peace. Sovereigntists on the Right argue that open borders invite migrants who take our jobs and introduce 'alien' cultural habits. They have also blamed open borders for terrorism. Sovereigntists on the Left see open borders as a factor behind cascading inequalities and 'casino' capitalism. And we have also seen heated discussion on whether we can have meaningful democracy and social policy in a polity with open borders and fuzzy (cosmopolitan or European) cultural identities.

At the centre of these discussions are always borders, which differentiate between insiders and outsiders, between the public and the private, and between rulers and subjects. Borders are not just lines on a map, but represent complex institutions determining the links between territory, authority, identity and rights. Some borders are formal, others informal; both can be sealed or porous to various degrees. Certain borders delineate private ownership while others demarcate public authority. And there are also 'symbolic' borders, separating virtual spaces where social groups or ideas congregate. These symbolic borders demarcate different 'sites of identification where the rudimentary aspects of our political and social identities are called into question, scrutinized and judged'.[4] We tend to focus on territorial borders, but as James W. Scott rightly argued, they should be 'understood as part of a much larger complex of regimes, practices and narratives that perform various border-making functions'.[5] Not everything in politics is about borders, but they are at the centre of much current contestation, for good and ill.

The more vulnerable borders become, the more stringent the efforts undertaken to reinforce them. Think about the walls around refugee camps, or biometric checks at airports. The more people and their money, goods, customs and ideas trespass borders, the more is done to recreate the local and to arrest these trans-border flows. Consider calls for trade protectionism or for curbing migration. These efforts to reinforce borders, physical or digital, may sound plausible to some of us, but are also futile because we are trying to seal borders precisely at a time when we seem least able to do so. And hence there is a growing disjuncture between symbolic and real politics. Although threats are becoming increasingly invisible, dispersed, networked and clandestine, we are constructing new barbed-wire walls. Although much communication, business and culture is moving into unbounded cyberspace, states are rushing to emphasize their territorial grip. Meanwhile, individuals active on digital social media are trying to recreate tribal identities there. Is this paradoxical situation novel, or are we simply repeating history?

Partitioning and allocating space

The opening of Stanley Kubrick's epic drama *2001: A Space Odyssey* visualized the prehistoric conquest of space by rival African tribes.[6] At stake in the movie was a waterhole crucial for the tribes' survival. However, humans attempt to acquire territory for a variety of reasons, some of them sincere and honest, others sinister and dishonest. Crucially, each claim to

a certain land, air or water leaves other humans dispossessed, generating conflicts.

Historically, the defence of claimed space has required legitimation and fortification. The articulation and protection of noble, if not sacred, ideals such as property, security or sovereignty seeks to achieve the former. Various sorts of walls, fences and barriers aim to achieve the latter. Whether fortified borders have ensured security better than dialogue, inter-dynastic marriages or disarmament, can be questioned. The defence of 'sacred' property rights has usually ignored the rights of indigenous people and other historically expropriated settlers. When those who affirm property rights do not live on the disputed piece of land, we are in an ambiguous moral realm adjudicating property claims. Consider 'land grabs' in Africa that allow firms to exploit natural resources, or the astronomical profits of real estate firms in mega-cities resulting from the manipulation of property prices. Sovereignty is also one of those sacred but much abused concepts, used to justify the prerogatives of nation-states – to use Stephen D. Krasner's words, 'an organized hypocrisy'.[7]

Different actors, public and private, use analogous means of partitioning and allocating territory. As A. John Simmons observed, 'Modern nation-states relate to their claimed territorial borders in many of the same ways in which individual landowners relate to their property lines. Both are in most cases permitted by applicable laws to fence (or wall) their holdings and otherwise govern movement of persons and things across their boundary lines.'[8] Open seas are only partly partitioned and allocated, and international laws prohibit the national appropriation of outer space and any sovereignty claims related to it. Outer space is the only 'province of all mankind' free from partitioning, but one wonders for how long, given the encroaching militarization of the cosmos.

Moreover, the cyberspace that refers to global computer networks is hardly a province of all mankind. Microsoft holds more than 90 per cent of the world market share of digital operating systems. States such as Russia and China claim the right to independently govern their internet public policies, free from any external interference. Artists demand intellectual property protection in cyberspace, with national courts adjudicating these claims. Defence against cyberattacks has led to the creation of borders in the online realm. Social scientists have also pointed to the 'everyday border-making narratives and practices' on the internet.[9] Social networking platforms such as Facebook and TikTok are full of niche groups and communities, where participants distinguish themselves from outsiders via their shared views or interests.

Since moral and even utilitarian justifications of bordering prove tricky, humans have tended to use legal means to justify the property rights of the individual and the sovereignty of states. Harsh law is better than no law, so goes the argument since the Roman era: *dura lex sed lex*. The law has not been able to do away with all ambiguities, however. Who is the owner of the apples from your tree that fall on the neighbour's side of the wall? Does the law about non-interference in the internal affairs of states apply to gross violations of human rights prohibited by the same law? Matters have become even more complicated in the internet era as online transactions take place across numerous jurisdictions with no detectible, let alone fixed, centre or location. Traditionally, courts have decided conflicts of law stemming from transnational interactions through deference to the principle of *lex loci delicti*, the law of the place in which the wrong was committed. In the geographically fluid environment of cyberspace, however, the place of the wrong is often not evident.

The fuzzy nature of frontiers, and even walls and fences, has obviously frustrated the quest for partitioning and allocating space. Sealing frontiers requires adequate technological and administrative capacities, lacking for the large part of human history. Constructed by the Roman emperor Hadrian, an 80-mile-long wall 'from sea to sea' separated the 'barbarians' from the Romans on the British Isles, but the dominant type of Roman border was much more flexible and imprecise. Roman *limes*, like Old French *marches*, represented a geographical zone rather than a clear line as was the case with Hadrian's Wall or the Antonine Wall in Scotland. Even the Great Wall of China was more a symbol of power than a real attempt to control all kinds of flows across the empire's territory. Walls surrounding medieval cities may have been effective in providing defence against intruders, but movements outside the walls of cities have usually been beyond anybody's firm control – until the ascendancy of nation-states. Inadequate (military) technology made it difficult to enforce any lines on the ground, but complex medieval governance systems made firm borders inappropriate and futile. As a distinguished American scholar, John Gerard Ruggie, explained:

> The medieval system of rule reflected 'a patchwork of overlapping and incomplete rights of government', which were 'inextricably superimposed and tangled', and in which

'different juridical instances were geographically interwoven and stratified, and plural allegiances, asymmetrical suzerainties and anomalous enclaves abounded'.[10]

The material possibilities for controlling large territories arrived only in the mid-nineteenth century with the advent of electricity, steel and steam. Nation-states were finally able to set and control borders to a remarkable degree. Yet the same technology that helped states to set boundaries could also be used to trespass over these borders. Present-day digital technologies are successfully utilized by border enforcement units and by migrants, and by investors and ideologues whose fortunes depend on the ability to cross borders.

Ordering and othering

Why do humans obsessively draw lines that divide the world into specific enclaves? Some of us may well be 'geographic beings' for whom the process of bordering 'seems natural' but, as Alexander C. Diener and Joshua Hagen rightly argue, borders are anything but natural; they exist 'only to the extent that humans regard them as meaningful'.[11] The survival instincts manifested in Kubrick's epic movie could well explain the purpose of bordering in prehistoric times, but does this logic equally apply to societies in the internet era? Perhaps we are lost in the mysterious digital universe and hang on to borders in order to shield us from galactic storms and gales.

What exactly is the purpose and meaning of borders? Why are we building them?

Two Dutch geographers, Henk van Houtum and Ton van Naerssen, have offered a concise and convincing answer to this question: bordering is about ordering and othering.[12] The former represents a political project of governance, the latter a political project of belonging. Governance presupposes wealth and security. This is why the advocates of borders talk about chaos, fear and crisis to castigate the idea of a borderless world. Belonging presupposes affinity, trust, safety and the recognition of being an important member of a given group. The advocates of borders talk in this context about threats of alien cultures intruding on our peaceful home or *heimat*, sometimes even violently in the case of terrorists. In other words, the guardians of borders offer fellow citizens communal bonds, law and order in exchange for power over them.

Borders affect not just minorities and migrants, but also mainstream tourists, traders, investors and broadcasters who make their living from trans-border exchanges of services, capital and labour. Even people who never leave their local area are affected, because the notion of sovereignty gives states the power to issue laws ordering the lives of all those within given borders. Citizens exchange their freedoms for a sense of authority and cultural identity, however illusory. Those who 'do not belong' can be stopped at the border or confronted with a long list of conditions determining their rights after crossing the border. The less fortunate are squashed in ghettos and detention camps with few ways to claim their rights, including the right to asylum. Many of us are familiar with the refugee camps in Turkey or Libya, demanded and financed by European governments.[13] However, sometimes refugees are able to 'claim' their own piece of land, as was the case of the Calais 'Jungle', occupied by refugees trying to cross the English Channel from France.[14]

Whether authority and cultural identity are illusory or real depends more on democracy, communication and culture than on borders. However, the guardians of borders assert that the former depend on the latter to some degree. In an open-ended space with no borders, prerequisites of democracy such as loyalty, accountability and representation may prove to be an empty shell. The acceptance of communal burdens such as taxes or military service is also difficult to envisage in a border-less society without cultural bonds and mutual trust. The Dutch commentator, Paul Scheffer, has made his anxiety loud and clear: 'The call for borders to be closed cannot be far away if all that liberals can come up with is an appeal for them to be open ... If freedom flourishes only within certain limits, might this borderless era presage a new absence of freedom? ... Can a democracy endure without borders?'[15]

I am rather puzzled by this anxiety because we have never truly had a borderless world. We only know a world with borders, albeit of different types; some hard and some soft, some containing vast territories of land and others comprising digital spaces. The borders of empires, states, counties and cities are different to those of ethnic neighbourhoods or gendered spaces. The European Union is trying to get rid of internal borders, but its external (Schengen) border is anything but open. Ordering and othering manifests itself differently in all these cases and obviously with different results. We can debate the pros and cons of different kinds of borders, but a completely borderless world is a straw man frequently used in political propaganda.

Borders are always manifestations of power for those inside and outside the dividing lines. They segregate not only people with different passports, but also people of different wealth, mobility, education, identity and status. However, borders can also create communities. People living in close proximity to borders often make their living by crossing them on a daily basis in search of jobs, goods and friends, and they form distinct trans-border communities of shared interests and loyalties. Even such a conflict-ridden frontier as between Israelis and Palestinians on the West Bank bears witness to the existence of trans-border communities, albeit communities of expediency rather than faith in this particular case.[16] Airports create another type of community. They are exceptionally fluid, but rely on a stable network of administrative and commercial services. Olga Tokarczuk, awarded the 2018 Nobel Prize in literature, considers airports a new type of city-state, with a fixed location, but ever-changing citizens. Constitutions of these new 'republics' are 'written on flight tickets', while boarding passes represent the 'identity cards of passengers'.[17]

Borders have a different meaning and importance for different groups of people. As long as there have been borders, there have been people using them as a protective shield, often against a second group – those determined to ignore and cross these shields for malign or noble purposes. I call the former 'settlers' and the latter 'nomads', while Peter Sloterdijk uses the terms 'cave and tree dwellers': 'For the one, it is the love of the shell that counts; for the other, the love of spaciousness.'[18] Settlers have usually viewed themselves as guardians of law, identity and order, but they have also been seen as guardians of unjust privileges, hierarchies and structures. Nomads have often conceived of themselves as envoys of freedom and progress, but they have also been called barbarians, colonizers and invaders.

It is often claimed that borders create advantaged insiders and disadvantaged outsiders; the former keep the latter at arm's length, unwilling to share their resources. But these categories sometimes make little sense. Economic autarchy made millions of people hungry in the Soviet Union. Ordinary Russian or Ukrainian 'insiders' felt imprisoned by the Soviet government, if only because they were unable to exit their impoverished country. The border was sealed for both outsiders and insiders. Millions of Soviet citizens were locked up in forced labour camps: *The Gulag Archipelago*, to use the title of Aleksandr Solzhenitsyn's famous work.[19] Colonial powers, on the other hand, may well look like outsiders to colonized populations, but they are anything but disadvantaged. Although colonial rulers frequently complained about the costs of empire, their policies of 'open borders' were aimed at generating selfish profits for the imperial centre rather than bringing civilization to 'barbarians'.[20] Besides, the openness of these borders was rather selective.

The very notion of insiders and outsiders is tricky because all of us are part of certain networks (states, professions, social groups), but strangers to others. There are also groups of people who struggle to identify with either category. Are second-generation migrants insiders or outsiders? What about detainees?

The urge to move across different kinds of borders can be a matter of personal choice, independent from political or economic circumstances. The protagonist of Tokarczuk's book *Bieguni* (published in English under the title *Flights*) spelled out her choice in the following way:

> Standing on the anti-flood shaft, watching the water current, I realized that despite all dangers, what's on the move is better than what's at rest; that nobler will be change than stability; that what's immobilized must disintegrate, degenerate and turn into dust, but what is moving will last forever.[21]

More often than not, however, nomads are products of the society they find themselves in. Refugees are driven out of their home country by war, famine and oppression. During the first two months of the Russian invasion of Ukraine, 5 million people, mostly women and children, fled to neighbouring states. Turkey is 'home' to some 4 million refugees and asylum seekers, most of them escaping atrocities in Syria. In the affluent West our choices are usually not determined by such extreme circumstances, and yet the motivation is the same. Fern, the key protagonist of the acclaimed 2020 movie *Nomadland*, superbly played by Frances McDormand, transformed from a settler to a nomad after she lost her husband and job, and could no longer afford to maintain a stable home. Like many others in her situation following the 2008 financial crash, she started to roam the country in a campervan looking for seasonal work. The movie features numerous representatives of this new American 'tribe', united by harsh circumstances, as well as friendship.

Ryan, the protagonist of the 2009 movie *Up in the Air*, played by George Clooney, undergoes the opposite transformation – from a nomad to a settler. Ryan works for a consultancy firm specialized in employment termination assistance. He constantly flies from one place to another, firing people with a smile and a motivational speech, encouraging desperate people to live free of burdensome relationships and material possessions tying them to any specific workplace. However, Ryan falls in love and his nomadic lifestyle threatens the developing relationship, hence the conversion hinted in the final sequence of the movie.

The term 'nomad' used to be associated with pastoral tribes moving around in search of wild plants and game. Today, it has acquired a new meaning and dimension. We now have numerous diverse categories of people moving around for personal or professional reasons. Some are fleeing war, oppression, economic hardship or environmental cataclysms, and others are forcibly displaced by their respective regimes. There are also groups of people for whom moving around is a chosen lifestyle, not necessarily caused by economic or political hardship. Most nomads are poor and distressed, but some nomads are rich and confident. Putting these diverse groups of people under a single label may be questioned, but it is not unusual in public discourse and academia. For instance, when we talk about a nation we do not assume that all co-nationals look alike. In fact, the group of settlers is also wide and diversified. Aristocratic landowners in the United Kingdom may have an attachment to their place just as redundant miners do, but they are clearly very different in other terms. We should also acknowledge that the categories of nomads and settlers are fuzzy rather than firm. Migrants of the second or third generation can oppose new generations of migrants because they compete for scarce social services and jobs. Misery is not necessarily conducive to solidarity. Wealthy people do not always stick together either.

According to the UN High Commissioner for Refugees (UNHCR), we currently have 82.4 million forcibly displaced people in the world, of whom more than a quarter are refugees (others are internally displaced). This number has doubled since 2010 and is higher now than it has ever been.[22] To this number we should add the unaccounted millions moving in search of a job like Fern, Bob and Swankie in *Nomadland*. Bulgaria, an EU member state, is a relatively affluent nation by global standards, and yet more Bulgarians are now working abroad than in Bulgaria itself.[23] Like nomads, they shuttle between their native country and Germany, the United Kingdom, Spain or Belgium, where they are able to work. The spread of evictions in the affluent part of the world mentioned earlier has also produced a community of homeless and jobless nomads. And there is also a rapidly growing group of 'digital nomads' who wander the world not only physically, but virtually. A firm called Nomads, promising to 'craft the ideas that circulate', with offices in Amsterdam, Dubai, London and Singapore, helps prominent clients such as National Geographic, Adidas, Rolls-Royce, Johnson & Johnson, Emirates and Airbnb to facilitate remote employment.[24] States are trying to attract digital nomads using tax breaks and visa offerings. According to a study by the Smart Working Observatory of Milan's Politecnico, remote workers in Italy increased from 570,000 in 2019 to 6.5 million during the spring 2020 lockdown.[25] The pandemic 'freed' many workers from their offices, and made many more wander the web, without leaving home.

For David Goodhart, a popular British commentator, nomads are chiefly privileged, highly educated people who benefit from open borders for capital, goods, services and labour. He calls them 'Anywheres' and contrasts them with 'Somewheres', who are less mobile and poorly adapted to a

world with porous borders. Anywheres are 'comfortable with immigration, European integration and the spread of human rights legislation' and see themselves as 'citizens of the world'.[26] Somewheres are 'more socially conservative and communitarian by instinct'. They are 'uncomfortable' with immigration, the 'reduced status of non-graduate employment' and 'more fluid gender roles'.[27]

Harvard professor Charles S. Maier talks about the 'limousine liberals of globalization (immune from foreign economic competition and facing little threat of unemployment)' and those who 'derive protection from borders and cherish national or ethnic identity (working for the administration or military)'.[28]

A similar dichotomy has been advanced by two prominent European academics, Ruud Koopmans and Michael Zürn. They talk about Communitarians and Cosmopolitans pitched against each other, like the political Right and Left in the past. Cosmopolitans (the neoliberal and leftish versions) advocate 'open borders, universal norms and supranational authority'. Communitarians (bigots, demagogues and xenophobes) defend 'border closure, cultural particularism and national sovereignty'.[29] The authors provide a sophisticated explanation of the sizeable cleavage between what I call nomads and settlers, but if the comments and cases I cited earlier are genuine, the 'border' dividing these two groups is fuzzy rather than hard and permanent. The pandemic illustrates this very well. It was often Cosmopolitans and Anywheres who supported lockdowns, while Communitarians and Somewheres wanted to move freely despite the associated dangers. Refugees also escape this simple classification. Are they reluctant Cosmopolitans or relocated Communitarians? These complications suggest that the struggle over borders is not set in stone, but on shifting sand. I am not sure we want to go from boundaries written in sand to those carved in stone, but even if the answer were positive, in a practical sense I would not know how to replace porous and impermanent borders with the impermeable and permanent.

The changing nature of borders

I have argued that borders represent complex institutions determining the links between territory, identity, authority and rights. If the latter categories undergo change, so must borders. Let me risk four general observations here. First, with physical territory losing importance, borders are moving to cyberspace and outer space. Second, with increased difficulties associated with controlling territorial borders, authorities are locating control in 'everyday spaces', to use John Allen's words, demanding identity documents before providing basic medical services, for instance.[30] Third, with identities becoming more fluid and multifaceted, borders tend to reflect a complex mosaic with no clear pattern. Fourth, the militant defence of our intimate spaces hardens the othering and proliferates conflicts, and so we live in isolated bubbles (Peter Sloterdijk) or filter bubbles (Eli Pariser), detached from each other and the real world.[31]

It is too early to grasp the implications of these transformations, but it looks like we are heading for a new kind of digital medievalism that replaces the existing system of sovereign territorial states. Instead of relatively fixed and hard territorial borders we are getting increasingly soft borders in a state of flux, including online and in outer space. The process of unbounding and re-bounding does not end, but acquires new and quite mysterious features.

Physical territory used to be a crucial economic and military asset, so it is little wonder that borders were chiefly about controlling 'strategic' terrains. Mountains, rivers and marshes represented valuable natural defences. Control over natural resources was crucial for industrial and agrarian production. None of this is obsolete, and geography still matters, but it is evident that physical territory has lost some of its importance with the explosion of digital economic transactions, and intercontinental ballistic missiles. The lives of many people are still determined by goods crossing physical borders, as the UK–EU squabble over the Irish border manifests, but for some time now economic fortunes are already being made on the internet. Soldiers still guard physical borders on land and water, but these borders are of limited utility against cyberattacks or nuclear threats. These soldiers cannot stop local floods and droughts caused by the global climate crisis. Some politicians may well be fond of physical walls and territorial defence units parading national flags, but one does not need to be an expert to appreciate that only some modern weapons, capital flows and even migrants can be arrested at the border proper.

It may therefore be rather banal to observe that borders are moving to cyber- and outer space with the advent of new technologies. However, this does not imply that we comprehend the implications of shifting borders to these underexplored spaces. Will the partitioning and allocating of cyber- and outer space represent a repetition of what we have done to the Earth and its territory? The narrative of the United States Space Command's mission sounds worryingly familiar:

Space enables our national security to preserve our way of life. From protecting the homeland and fighting our nation's wars alongside allies and partners, to providing humanitarian assistance, space makes the achievements of America's military possible.[32]

Not only do China and Russia reason in a similar way, but so do all forty different states who at present have their own national space agencies. Private companies are also contemplating the 'colonization' of the mineral-rich solar system and the 'privatization of the final frontier', to use Stewart Patrick's words.[33] Two researchers from the Canadian University of British Columbia have documented an unprecedented increase in private satellites deployed in the low-Earth orbit (LEO). Between 2019 and 2021 the number of active and defunct satellites in LEO increased by over 50 per cent, to about 5,000. SpaceX, owned by Elon Musk, is on track to add 11,000 more as it builds its Starlink mega-constellation. Musk has already filed for permission for another 30,000 satellites with the US Federal Communications Commission. Amazon, OneWeb, Telesat and the Chinese state-owned company GW all have similar plans.[34]

Efforts to partition, allocate and control cyberspace are also advancing, for a variety of reasons – both noble and sinister. The 2021 Russian security strategy talks about 'defending sovereignty in the digital information space' to protect the country from foreign digital penetration, and especially from the spread of alien ideas.[35] Policy to introduce the digital taxation of large tech companies is hopefully being guided by nobler considerations, but these plans are often portrayed as discriminatory vis-à-vis small states such as Ireland and Hungary, and as unsuited for consumer-facing digital businesses.[36] Clearly, we are in uncharted territory here.

Cyberspace has gained importance, but the importance of physical space has not diminished. Political actors operate in both spaces, albeit often with different priorities and capabilities. Russia's invasion of Ukraine and the EU's response are good examples here. Russia operates in Ukraine using chiefly conventional weapons on the ground and simultaneously conducts a propaganda campaign through digital social platforms blaming the EU and NATO for the war. The EU does not even have an army, but it urged member states to send weapons to Ukraine. At the same time the EU 'bombarded' Russia with sanctions targeting Russian digital financial transactions. Bank accounts of numerous Russian institutions and prominent individuals were frozen, and Russian banks were removed from the messaging system that enables digital international payments, the so-called SWIFT. These sanctions were aimed at crippling Russia's economy in order to stop attacks on Ukrainian territory, but in due time they may also lead to a regime change in Moscow.

Another observation concerns the changing nature of traditional territorial state borders. The movement of people, goods, services and labour is increasingly difficult to control at these frontiers. For instance, most people 'illegally' residing (and working) in Europe arrived legally and stayed on after their valid visa expired. This has prompted states to extend 'border' controls across the entire territory of their respective countries, obliging institutions as well as ordinary citizens to perform controlling functions. Medical doctors and hospital staff, university professors and schoolteachers, landlords and estate agents, public officials and private bank employees have been obliged to demand proof of identity and lawful status from patients, students, tenants and clients. Failure to comply with these laws is threatened by penalties. In this way border controls have encroached on the everyday life of citizens and entered everyday spaces. Borders can now be located everywhere, and each citizen may be forced to perform border checks at their school or hospital. As the scandal related to the Windrush generation in the United Kingdom demonstrated, the definition of an 'illegal' person, deprived of basic social and legal rights, can be abused by politicians and the civil service – in some cases, with citizens' acquiescence.[37]

Border controls are also performed in places far away from where potential travellers may depart. The biometric tests and pre-screening of flight passengers, performed by foreign consulates, local administrations and air companies, is a good example of shifting border controls away from territorial borders proper.[38] Initially these extensive forms of control were applied with suspected terrorists in mind, but they have since become a widespread practice targeting everyday commuters.

Whether these practices curb or defend our freedom is viewed differently by nomads and settlers.[39] However, it is hard to resist the impression that the administration of borders is gradually shifting from the public to the private sphere. This brings us to the topic of identity boundaries.

Caves, bubbles and echo chambers

Identities have always been in flux, and this could not but influence the nature of borders, which are in essence about ordering and othering. States have claimed that their borders not only demarcate distinct administrations, but also different nations. However, many states are multinational, and some nations live in more than one state. You may even argue that states such as Israel fit both these categories. Moreover, national identity is but one of many other identities, and not necessarily the most dominant, as claimed by nativists. Sociologists have pointed to a remarkable proliferation of different types of identities in recent years, especially those personally adopted or chosen as opposed to those unchosen.[40] Sociologists have also highlighted the increased policing of these identities, which relates to ordering and othering in the context of our discussion. As Rogers Brubaker observed, we witness:

the massive destabilization of long taken-for-granted categorical frameworks, which has significantly enlarged the scope for choice and self-fashioning in the domains of race, ethnicity, sex, gender, and sexuality. Anxieties about opportunistic, exploitative, or fraudulent identity claims have generated efforts to 'police' unorthodox claims – as well as efforts to defend such claims *against* policing – in the name of authentic, objective, and unchosen identities.[41]

These cultural squabbles are sometimes linked to a specific state territory, especially when national courts are involved, but more often than not they are transnational and conducted in the digital space through social media. This is where militant bordering is most frequent and fanatic, although this does not apply to all social media sites.

Students of politics tend to emphasize identity conflicts caused by migration and thus related to the crossing of traditional state borders. A cultural clash between Muslim migrants and the liberal societies of the countries hosting them is emphasized in these discussions.[42] Yet the cultural clash between fundamentalist and moderate Catholics in Poland is no less fierce than that between Liberals in Holland and the Dutch of (Muslim) Moroccan origin. A battle for and against the rights of the LGBT+ community is now engulfing numerous countries and has become truly transnational. Some Muslim migrants in France may be hostile towards LGBT+ people, but so are some local French citizens; in Hungary the anti-LGBT+ militant squads contain only native Hungarians!

There is a tendency to view identity conflicts in bipolar terms: (religious) conservatives versus (secular) progressives, or populists versus liberals. I find this black-and-white thinking inaccurate where identities are concerned. Women demanding the liberalization of restrictions on legal abortion are not necessarily supportive of transgender rights. Some lesbians and gay men are religious, while some ethnic minorities vote for xenophobic parties. Identity is about personal feelings and, with the rise of identity politics, ordering and othering becomes multifaceted. This leads to a complex mosaic of fluid cultural borders with no clear shape. Attempts to map identity are awkward because cartography is not good at grasping cultural nuances.

Although identity conflicts are bread-and-butter politics, they usually concern intimate issues such as race, sexuality or gender. The discrimination against and abuse towards racial and sexual minorities creates a feeling of vulnerability among these communities. Also vulnerable are children abused by priests, or women mistreated by their husbands, and they seek protection. Hence, the concept of safe spaces has gained prominence in recent years; safe space implying that vulnerable individuals can share their experiences without external interference and talk about ways of shielding themselves from marginalization, harassment, hate speech and violence. Claims to safe spaces on university campuses have met resistance, however, after some prominent speakers were disinvited by students unwilling to face different or controversial opinions. A petition to the University of Cardiff to cancel a lecture by the famous feminist writer, Germaine Greer, because of her alleged 'misogynist views towards trans women' was widely discussed in the United Kingdom and Australia, Greer's native country.[43] The discussion was not so much about trans women, but about open versus closed identity borders in public spaces. President Obama himself argued against safe spaces on campuses in a speech at Howard University, a symbolic place for African-American students.[44] That said, demands for safe spaces have formally been recognized by many institutions and even states. In 2019 the Safe Spaces Act was signed into law in the Philippines, for instance.

In cyberspace, identity borders are set without much public oversight and these borders are also, in most cases, pretty hard. Social media can expose individuals to facts and opinions which challenge their partisan beliefs, especially when their online networks are comprised of diverse individuals.[45] Quite often, however, users of social media platforms respond like the students in Cardiff; they are keen to converse with people who share rather than oppose their views. Media specialists use the term 'echo chambers', referring to situations in which beliefs are amplified by communication inside a closed circle and insulated from criticism. Social media algorithms which target users with similar views or behaviours can reinforce the closed circulation of information and communication. Selective exposure, contagion and group polarization are the most cited outcomes of such communication bubbles and echo chambers. Identity borders are hardened as a result, and in some cases informed by conspiracies and post-truth.[46]

The danger of finding yourself insulated from a variety of points of view was grasped long ago by Plato, in his Parable of the Cave.[47] Imagine, says Plato, a cave in which prisoners are chained in such a way that all they can see are shadows thrown on a wall in front of them. All they know of life are these shadows, consequently if a prisoner were freed, he would realize how limited his vision was in the cave. Plato would not feel comfortable in contemporary echo chambers and bubbles as, according to him, truth can only be found by escaping them. Yet for Peter Sloterdijk, a contemporary German philosopher, bubbles are as natural for people as wombs are for foetuses.[48] We need intimate spaces where we can find security and affinity in the complex universe. Bubbles do not exclude solidarity and communication, according to Sloterdijk, but I am not sure what kind of ordering and othering bubbles imply, especially on social media. There has been little dialogue, let alone solidarity, between the liberal and the extreme-right bubbles, nor between feminist and misogynist ones.[49] For these contrasting identity groups, a compromise would imply a betrayal of their deeply ingrained sense of self. Is there any point in a dialogue with misogynists propagating hate? Can one expect victims of a foreign invasion to engage in dialogue with their slaughterers? Some argue that you should even converse with abusers, if only to understand their motivations, but the utility of such efforts can be questioned.

The ordering and othering practised on digital social media echoes the nationalist discourse of a century or two ago. As Ernest Gellner brilliantly observed:

Nationalism is not a shapeless free-floating unspecific unfocused feeling, like some nameless elusive *Angst*. Its object is normally only too sharply defined, as the love of certain categories of people, and the detestation of others . . . God help you if you find yourself with the wrong face, colour or accent in a mob possessed by nationalist hysteria.[50]

Contemporary nativists, like their famous or infamous ancestors, insist that only nations (for some, holy nations) can organize societies and make states work. They also try to polarize political discourse and reduce it to the choice between good and evil, us and them. Yet, unlike their ancestors, contemporary nativists can hardly control the means of communication, and they encounter societies that rally under national flags during sporting events, but not on other days of the year. As the *Observer* columnist, Kenan Malik, explained during the Euro 2020 football championship:

Sport generates a kind of tribalism I would not wish to replicate outside the stadium. It is fierce and unforgiving, a loyalty that bears no rational scrutiny . . . I will cheer on England with fervour and fury. But after those 90 minutes are up, my Englishness will fade into the background. I am tribal about sport, not about the nation.[51]

Malik's views are not shared by all English people, Boris Johnson among them, I suspect. Students who signed the petition in Cardiff mentioned earlier may well agree with Malik, but they proved tribal in a different identity squabble. Each tribe tries to set its own border and enlarge its 'safe' space. This is the essence of tribal politics conducted by agents with a fixed sense of identity. Yet the plurality of identity claims and of the means of communication make it difficult for any of the tribes to dominate. The point here is not to try and establish which tribe is virtuous and correct, but to show the complex mosaic of identity-related borders.[52] Yet it is hard to ignore the paradox of our era: the more diversified and plural identities are, the more efforts are being made to simplify, harden and seal them. Students of conservative thought may argue that this paradox is not new. Conservatism was always about resisting changes in our cultural and political preferences. Fixing identity borders and denying progress was part of its agenda. We may point to the futility of this agenda, but this does not imply the end of nostalgic politics. Different strands of progressive thinking rise and die, but conservatism seems to be always in vogue.

If ordering and othering is part of human nature, we can forget about the vision of a borderless world. In fact, I wonder whether we can prosper without a certain degree of order. Othering even makes moral sense in some situations. Perpetrators of violence and those who incite it ought to be named and shamed, if not punished. The question, therefore, is what kind of borders we endorse or condemn. Borders can be conceived of as a meeting point between different cultures or as an intersection between two administrative regimes. But they can also represent a separation point: a place where we say goodbye to our 'home' with no certainty of ever going back. The 'other' on the other side of the border, territorial or digital, can be welcoming or hostile, curious or arrogant, tolerant or dogmatic. The ordering on 'our' or 'their' side of the border can be rigid or flexible, liberating or oppressive, responsive or hierarchical.

Paulina Ochoa Espejo, an American scholar of Mexican origin, argued that conceiving borders as the limits of identity groups results in a 'desert island' model of borders; each group aspires to its own unified and clearly delimited space. The alternative Ochoa Espejo proposes is a 'watershed' model of borders that gives priority to jurisdictions and places rather than identity and belonging. Unlike a desert island, watersheds are connected and interdependent, because it is hard to determine exclusive ownership of flowing water. Her model thus envisages interconnected systems where institutions, people and the natural environment together create overlapping civic duties and relations. The global climate emergency makes the native/alien divide outdated and dangerous, she argues.[53]

I am not sure we will be able to get rid of identity politics, but I agree with Ochoa Espejo that borders should protect places and not just the people inhabiting them. Perhaps climate change, with its devastating implications, may impel the creation of trans-border bonds to preserve the natural environment. Does this sound overly optimistic? Probably so, unless we comprehend that calls to 'take back control of our borders' are intended to establish control over us, no matter which identity bubble we currently live in.

4

HIGH-SPEED REGIMES

Have you been running short of breath lately, shuttling between the office, school, home, gym and local community gatherings? Have you been answering emails on the sofa after dinner, talking to colleagues on hands-free whilst rushing to collect your kids from school? Have you felt as though you were failing your partner, kids, parents, friends and community, while doing the minimum your boss required? Have you spent hours on trains, in airports or in rush-hour traffic? Welcome to the modern version of time-and-space-compressing democracy and capitalism!

Yes, like many of us I agree that we all should slow down, travel less and set aside more time for family, cultural activities, community participation or political engagement. Yet when Covid-19-related policies froze our time and space, many of us suffered, and some of us rebelled against the lockdowns and other restrictions. Standing still will not bring about a better future, not to mention that we need to pay our

bills in the meantime. The question is: can we move forward at a speed that will not cause a crash? The answer depends on our understanding of the roots, manifestations and implications of speed. Rapid acceleration is a shock to our political and economic systems. Adjusting to a 'high-speed society', to use the title of Hartmut Rosa and William E. Scheuerman's book, is also a painful process for many of us personally. However, change caused by acceleration is the endemic human condition.[1] We can try to resist, or to steer it. Benign neglect is arguably the least appealing option. Let's try to grapple with dilemmas related to 24/7 capitalism and democracy. Our political regimes run at high speed in emergency mode from one crisis to another with little reflection, transparency, deliberation or citizens' input. The implications of this permanent rush for our lives, work and democratic rights are tremendous, as I will try to show in this chapter.[2]

Accelerating change

There is no doubt that we live, commute and work at an ever-faster tempo. Capitalism and democracy are operating more rapidly – if not frantically – and changes in cultural habits are progressing at an increasing pace. Athletes run faster; fashion, diet and music alternate wildly; we even think, speak and write more quickly, albeit in bits and bytes full of acronyms. There are now courses in speed-reading and thinking to help us perform better. My favourite example is kwiklearning.com, which offers three-part 'Brain Trainings' allegedly used in more than 150 countries around the world. The firm seduces potential customers by coaxing: 'Accelerate your learning and life with our speed-reading and memory training designed for busy people and organizations who want to achieve more in less time.'[3]

The recent pandemic may have arrested the acceleration of the pace of our life, but technological acceleration only intensified as most of us became dependent on fast internet connections to go about our daily lives. Before the pandemic, I hardly ever used to shop online and I avoided online conferences. Today, these practices represent 'the new normal', even though most restrictions on our movements have abated.

For some of us, acceleration is a common human condition; for others it represents a brutal external intervention in the natural course of life. For some, acceleration is a curse, while for others it is a blessing. These judgements are often guided by acquired skills rather than philosophical reflections: my parents never learned to use computers and mobile devices, while my children can hardly function without them.

Acceleration is difficult to define and measure; for some it is 'just about everything', but serious scholars such as Hartmut Rosa point to three distinct dimensions of the phenomenon: (i) technological acceleration; (ii) acceleration of social change; and (iii) acceleration of the pace of life.[4] Rosa and other authors also point out that over the course of history we have had moments of deceleration. Scientists therefore argue over whether history indeed accelerates, or whether we only have episodes of acceleration in history. Whether acceleration *within* society is followed by the acceleration *of* society is also debated. The latter would imply speed-induced changes of attitudes and values resulting in new social structures and hierarchies. The cleavage between groups that are speed-ignorant and speed-savvy could outshine traditional cleavages based on gender, race or class.

The challenge is not only to catch up with those who are faster. Since speed compresses space, we also need to cope with the ensuing spatial dislocation. A growing tension between people rooted in a specific community and those who are mobile, if not placeless, is a vivid manifestation of the challenge caused partly by speed. Speed rewards networks more than traditional rigid structures, and hence the pressure to adjust our modes of public governance. The tension between territorial nation-states and global cities, discussed earlier, exemplifies the challenge caused by the power of accelerating networks.

Challenges, however serious, are not necessarily the reason for embracing fatalistic scenarios predominant in the literature on acceleration and high speed. For such different authors as Paul Virilio, Jeremy Rifkin or Carmen Leccardi, acceleration represents a highly risky, uncontrollable and irresponsible intervention in our natural setting that is destined to cause human suffering, possibly leading to 'the liquidation of the world'.[5] These worst-case scenarios may indeed materialize, but we cannot base our planning on them. Yes, travelling fast can lead to a crash, but only under certain conditions. And it is hard to deny the numerous advantages of fast travel. High-speed communication does not necessarily make us thoughtless, regardless of all the pitfalls of cyber capitalism; accelerated work does not always lead to enslavement; and life-saving medicines can't come soon enough. Protecting our natural environment may actually require more, rather than fewer, technological solutions, and speed will be crucial in achieving any success in this domain. We need to understand the factors causing the acceleration. The next step is to consider the pros and cons of high speed with the use of collective wisdom.

Causes of speed

Ever newer and faster technology is the most obvious factor behind social acceleration. Trains, cars and aircraft sped up travel, initially for the few, but gradually for everyone. We may rightly complain about traffic jams and ask why trains are underutilized. Yet it is hard to deny that cars have not only sped up, but also facilitated the lives of a great majority of people, despite all their downsides. In Oxford and Amsterdam I only use a bike, but in the hilly Tuscan countryside I cannot do without a car because the closest shop is a few miles away and there is no public transport. Air traffic is rightly under fire for enhancing air pollution; however, the spread of low-cost airlines has had an enormous emancipatory, if not equalizing, effect on millions of people. Suddenly, people who were not wealthy could enjoy the benefits of fast travel to places they knew only from TV soap operas and commercials.

Television is also a mixed blessing. It has accelerated (and spread) information, but also prejudices and fake news. (The telegraph and radio had a similar effect.) The internet was perhaps the most spectacular leap towards high-speed communication, with mixed results once again. The world has effectively been transformed into a 'global virtual village' over the past three decades thanks to digital technology. Sending a message or money to a distant location five centuries ago could take several days if not months; now it takes a fraction of a second. More crucially, the fusion of social media and internet communication has created 'a culture of endless construction and deconstruction', to use Manuel Castells' words – 'a polity geared towards the instant processing of new values and public moods'.[6] While we are still trying to comprehend the effects of digital high-speed communication, the internet continues to grow in size, beyond imagination.

Uncritically embracing techno-optimism may well be naive, but so is resisting technological progress. Besides, technology does not fall from the sky. Inventions and applications of technology need to be encouraged and financed. This brings us to capitalism as the frequently mentioned 'culprit' causing social acceleration and human suffering. As Ben Agger phrased it, 'speeding up fast capitalism' commits 'time robbery', depriving people of 'sleep, affect, family, leisure, nature, self and identity'.[7] Capitalism's quest for fast profits and quick turnover is certainly behind the spread of ever-new technologies accelerating our work, consumption and leisure. But this does not mean that we should uncritically embrace economic determinism, because non-economic factors behind speed are also important and ever present.

Students of culture point to secularism rather than capitalism as the reason for this ongoing acceleration. When people contemplate that there is nothing after death, they want to accomplish as much as possible in their relatively short life on Earth. No time to waste, is the message, and so we need to hurry. In 2019, when my local football club, Fiorentina, was purchased by the Italian-American billionaire, Rocco Commisso, his initial slogan was telling: Fast, Fast, Fast! His explanation was simple, but genuine: a man who has turned 70 has little time to win a much-desired trophy. But even Fiorentina's much younger supporters concurred with this statement.

Competition between humans, and earlier between humans and animals, can also explain our quest for speed and acceleration. A telling symbol of this competition was reproduced in Western movies such as *Last Train from Gun Hill* featuring Kirk Douglas and Anthony Quinn, or *The Good, the Bad and the Ugly* starring (a young) Clint Eastwood. The speediest (not necessarily the wisest or nicest) shooter has always prevailed in the movies that formed the worldview of post-Second World War generations, not just in the United States and Europe. Competition is obviously pronounced in economics, but speed also determines our social status, in education most notably. The quicker we graduate, the smoother we travel through life. Human instincts such as insecurity, jealousy or greed can also explain our rush; even if we are not competitive or greedy, we fear being left behind, and so we hurry.

Speed-generating technology is often produced and applied by the military sector, but again, there is no need to suspect sinister objectives here. Defence requirements and the quest for security, real or imagined, are often reasons for investing in ever-faster military technology. If machine guns and ballistic missiles are put at the service of an imperial conquest this is usually caused by political rather than technological developments. High-speed military technologies often find noble usage in the civilian sphere; the internet itself, which today assists the lives of the majority of people on Earth, was originally funded by the US Department of Defense to allow multiple computers to communicate in the event of nuclear war.

Acceleration certainly intensified in the nineteenth century with the spread of the telegraph and railways, and then again at the end of the twentieth century with the spread of the internet. However, technological advances generated speed long before the advent of capitalism (or, if you wish, before the Industrial and Neoliberal Revolutions), which suggests many different factors are at play here. I used to take visitors to the Cave di Maiano on the outskirts of Florence where Leonardo da Vinci allegedly tested man-made wings for humans to fly. It is hard to argue that Leonardo was an agent of capitalism. Perhaps he was just curious.

We are often told that high-speed social communication on the internet is perverting our language if not our thinking. Yet when I look at the SMS and WhatsApp messages of my children, I cannot but recall my university study of medieval manuscripts five decades earlier. These manuscripts were also full of mysterious abbreviations that could only be understood with the help of special Latin dictionaries such as the 1912 *Lexicon abbreviaturarum* by Adriano Cappelli. Medieval monks working on legal and canonical manuscripts were not necessarily in a hurry, but papyrus was expensive and in short supply and therefore they could not afford to write full words and sentences. Contemporary youngsters have plenty of space on their mobiles, but they demand instantaneous communication and hence the revival of abbreviations and the use of GIFs and emojis as a way to communicate faster.

Acronyms and abbreviations are also experiencing a renaissance in novels and movies. The BBC, which aired one of the

most popular crime dramas of the last decade, *Line of Duty*, was bombarded by viewers' complaints about the excessive use of baffling acronyms by the cast. Even Google was initially of no help to viewers desperately trying to discover the meaning of such abbreviations as CHIS (Covert Human Intelligence Source) or OCG (Organized Crime Group). Happily, there are now internet sites for decoding the most frequently used acronyms in this acclaimed television series.[8] These, and the online Urban Dictionary,[9] which decodes modern slang and abbreviations, represent a modern version of Cappelli's *Lexicon abbreviaturarum*.

24/7 work

Acceleration and speed affect our work in various ways. We are not only expected to work faster, but also longer, if not around the clock. Technology can accelerate our output, but it can also render us hostage to employers' demands in a manner unknown two or three decades ago. Speed goes hand in hand with flexibility and connectivity. We are expected to be online continuously and adjust to various types of instructions. When, in 1980, Frank Sinatra sang of the city that never sleeps, he was referring to New York, which was the city that pioneered the 24/7 subway system. Today, numerous services, supermarkets, ATMs, petrol stations and even dating hubs and locations of worship operate around the clock in most parts of the world. When we add to this the incessant operation of online communication, entertainment and commerce, the seemingly bizarre term coined by Manuel Castells, 'timeless time', acquires a tangible meaning.[10]

24/7 work is partly generated by consumer demand. We often want to shop late in the evening, even on Sundays, and we expect petrol stations to be open continuously. There is some suspicion, however, that owners of supermarket chains or petrol stations artificially create this consumer demand. And you do not need to be a Communist to feel that many companies treat our time and space as economic commodities that ought to be available around the clock. Of course, we can stand up to our employers, but we are ever less unionized in the cyber capitalist system, dominated by firms owned by anonymous shareholders and scattered all over the world. When our trade union representatives are granted an 'audience' with employers they are usually told that slowing down and reducing the territorial reach of their firm would put them out of business and employees out of a job.

Individual employers did not invent 24/7 capitalism, which operates around the clock from multiple locations. Employers simply adjusted their firms to technological changes, transnational competition and the changing value of goods, services and labour. Some of us still remember workers' struggles against clock discipline in factories, but today the clock is less and less in use. We are simply supposed to be available for work regardless of time and location. The distinction between work and leisure is effectively blurred, both in spatial and temporal terms. Homes, airports, gardens and cars have become the sites from which many of us perform work. As John Naughton put it: 'We are all sleeping in the office now.'[11] To make things worse, some of us are monitored by ActivTrak or similar 'spying' devices on our laptops or mobile phones, which means that employers have effectively invaded private homes, cars and gardens. Not only are our traditional struggles for limited working hours increasingly irrelevant, but so are those for statutory retirement age and for the duration of our contracts. Jobs tied to a specific location and time are becoming a relic of the outdated form of capitalism that we know from the works of Karl Marx. What *is* new, according to Jonathan Crary:

is the sweeping abandonment of the pretence that time is coupled to any long-term undertakings, even to fantasies of 'progress' or development. An illuminated 24/7 world without shadows is the final capitalist mirage of post-history, of an exorcism of the otherness that is the motor of historical change . . . 24/7 renders plausible, even normal, the idea of working without pause, without limits . . . without sleep.[12]

'Flexible' work from home (WFH) is the latest incarnation of 24/7 labour. Initially, not only workers but also employers felt uneasy about WFH, but the experience of pandemic seemed to change their minds. A 2021 poll by the recruiter Robert Half showed that 89 per cent of firms expected some form of hybrid working to become permanent after the Covid pandemic.[13] WFH could save employers some of the rental costs for offices with no reduction in the effective hours of work performed by employees. (Preliminary studies show that employees work longer hours under the WFH system.) Employees themselves are more divided, but not sceptical of WFH altogether. According to a survey by the Boston Consulting Group, 53 per cent of workers would prefer a hybrid model in the future.[14] We may well be spared commuting to the office and putting up with difficult colleagues by WFH, and flexibility in the hours of work can make childcare easier too.

Workcation is another popular incarnation of flexible 24/7 labour. A rapidly growing community of supporters believes that a workcation takes all the best bits of work and vacations and neatly combines them into one nomadic experience, as discussed earlier. Why should we do our work from home if we can do it from the most stunning touristic locations? 'We know that putting people in different environments, such as being close to nature, can make you more creative. It makes you less stressed,' Libby Sander from Bond Business School in Australia told the BBC.[15] Whether breaking the balance between work and leisure indeed makes most of us relaxed and happy remains to be tested. In the meantime, numerous hotels are already adjusting their services to the new customers' 'demand' and advertisements for workcations proliferate, featuring images of happy customers with a laptop on their knees on sunny beaches or in a rainforest. 'Stuck in the Hustle and Bustle of the IT city! Finally, we got you a perfect solution, in Gokarna. Idyllic beaches, picturesque temples, serene surroundings', promises one of the adverts.[16]

In the industrial era, the system of work reflected the principles of predictability, synchronization and planning, organized according to the clock. In the digital era, the system of work reflects the principles of flexibility, diversity and improvisation, grounded in instantaneous communication. The outcome of our work is now more important than the time of work, which paradoxically brings us back to the medieval task-oriented system of labour. In the emerging flexible and hybrid system, the distinction between work and leisure gets blurred, workers' rights and obligations are under-defined, while stable career patterns are illusory. We are supposed to adjust our work to the incessant flow of messages from our managers. Since rewards are based on the outcomes and not the duration of performance, there is a premium for self-discipline.

This system has numerous drawbacks. Our freedom to organize our work is often illusory. Women feel trapped when trying to combine working from home with childcare.[17] The erosion of stable career patterns is frequently to the disadvantage of older employees. Self-discipline does not suit everybody and pressures emerging from 24/7 work are often a source of stress rather than happiness (the latter reported by the *Economist!*).[18] However, we should not idealize the previous system with its mechanical, often senseless clock discipline. It is enough to read the 1967 essay of E.P. Thompson – 'Time, Work-Discipline, and Industrial Capitalism' – to cure oneself of a longing for the old, orderly, predictable and monotonous system.[19] Or, one can watch Charlie Chaplin's 1936 movie *Modern Times*, epitomizing the depressing absurdity of the mechanical work system. Bob Jessop may well be right to argue that fast capitalism meshes poorly with the fundamental rhythms of human existence, but I wonder whether slow capitalism meshes any better.[20] What is slow capitalism anyway?

High-speed democracy

We are only just starting to comprehend the implications for work in the new superfast digital economy. We should first identify opportunities and threats generated by a high-speed context. The next obvious task is to enhance the former, while constraining the latter, which brings us to the topic of democracy in the hectic environment of today.

Cynics would argue that politicians cannot control markets, which rapidly and ceaselessly operate across borders in a way that is neither transparent nor structured. But, in general, the objective is not necessarily to slow down capitalism and reduce its territorial reach. We first need to have a democratic discourse about the implications of speed and a few simple measures to protect us from pathological manifestations of turbo-capitalism. For instance, the European Parliament has called on the EU Commission to put forward a legislative proposal guaranteeing the right of workers to disconnect outside working hours – without facing consequences from their employers.[21] If transformed into law, this measure could represent an important protective shield against the excesses of the 24/7 high-speed economy. The problem is that democracy itself is also frantic, and it may fail to deliver on even modest expectations.

It is generally accepted by now that the unbounding of democratic spaces has challenged public institutions. When capital, goods, services and labour cross borders with relative ease, territorially bounded democratic institutions struggle to transform citizens' preferences into tangible policies. However, it is much less appreciated that the evolving nature of time has as important an impact on democracy as the evolving nature of space. To quote Régis Debray, a well-known French philosopher and political activist: 'Time is to politics what space is to geometry.'[22] Democratic institutions created in a society operating at a certain speed need palpable adjustments to cope with the accelerated pace of life, work, communication and business. All kinds of institutions, including democratic ones, are time-loaded and context-dependent. According to Robert Hassan, the 200-year-old 'nexus between capitalism, clock time and liberal democracy' was effectively destroyed with the internet revolution, generating a new, high-speed society.[23] We do not know what the new nexus between cyber capitalism, instantaneous time and post-liberal democracy will look like, but we know that numerous challenges abound.

Part of the problem is that the short-term horizons of profit-driven, neoliberal economics have made it difficult for democratic institutions to implement any ambitious, long-term projects – in effect confining them to quick, futile fixes. Another related problem stems from the fact that existing democratic institutions rely on time-consuming deliberation, negotiation and adjudication. With little time for democratic deliberation, it is hard to come to any satisfying decisions. Courts also need time to reflect on individual cases before they issue any authoritative judgments. Rushed negotiations between parties representing diverse interests generate few durable compromises. Creating and sustaining a sound social contract requires stability and constancy, and not relentless, rushed changes.

Citizens' participation in a high-speed society may also prove illusory, regardless of all the technological devices facilitating communication. As one of the most respected political scientists, Giovanni Sartori of Columbia University, put it: 'real democracy can only be, and must be, participatory democracy'.[24] However, in high-speed society many citizens feel far too busy to engage in public affairs and exercise their democratic citizenship. Some of them even consider voting a waste of time. This is partly because making sense of fast-moving events is difficult even for experts – let alone for ordinary voters who in a democracy are supposed to have the ultimate (sovereign) say.

The democratic institutions that we have inherited from the past reflect a difficult balance between the principles of rationality and efficiency. (Rational, but poorly implemented, policies are as bad as well-organized, but irrational, ones.) The legislature and the judiciary have been chiefly responsible for delivering the rationality of a given polity by carefully considering alternative policy options, creating universally applied laws, and making sure that the rule of law prevails. The executive has been chiefly responsible for delivering efficiency, which is more about doing rather than talking and thinking. Crisis management is the speciality of the executive because during crises there is little time for prolonged parliamentary or judicial research and deliberation. In a relatively static period between crises, the legislature adjusts the existing laws and the judiciary tries to undo the abuses of power committed during the last crisis.

In a high-speed society the balance between rationality and efficiency is destroyed because politics is chiefly about perpetual crisis management with little time for breaks and lengthy deliberation. The significance of the executive branch of the government increases during an endless crisis, while parliaments and courts are portrayed as stumbling blocks on the way to recovery. Politics resembles a permanent state of emergency with decisions taken in a hurry by the executive branch with little public input and time for reflection.[25] Parliaments and courts are increasingly marginalized or even contested by the executive. Success in such an emergency decision-making process results from sheer luck rather than purpose, logic and evidence. The success of Boris Johnson's zig-zag policy to combat Covid-19 is a good example of luck rather than wisdom.

As William Scheuerman rightly argued, the liberal democracy of the past several decades was 'reasoned, deliberative and reflective and thus dependent on slow rather than fast passage of time'.[26] The present day acceleration and time compression perverts democratic procedures and leads to the ruling by decree of a small group of ruling-party politicians in charge of the executive branch of the government. Incessant time pressure leaves little room for research, negotiation and compromise. Politics operates along the ideological blueprints of those in charge of the government and any kind of dissent is labelled as a betrayal of national interests bordering on subversion. Decisions taken are not only irrational in most cases, but they are also adopted in an autocratic manner, 'justified' by the real or imagined state of emergency.[27] Citizens are helpless objects of governmental policies with no input, nor even voice. Thus the notion of politics *for* rather than *by* the people prevails. And since we instantly move from one crisis to another with no 'slow' periods for reflection and the correction of mistakes, the policy process leads to outcomes that are not only irrational, but also utterly ineffective in most cases.

Populism is a child of 'a pathology of instantaneous democracy', argues Ming-Sung Kuo from the University of Warwick School of Law.[28] In his view, constitutional democracy assumes temporal gaps between formal decision-making stages, and also between opinion formation and policy-making. Unmediated politics at the expense of democratic representation and deliberation 'breathes new life to populism', because it allows populists to 'disrupt the multistage formal decision-making process [and] go unchecked easily'.[29] The French philosopher, Paul Virilio, goes even further and boldly declares: 'The more speed increases, the faster freedom decreases.'[30]

Should we slow down?

The multiple negative implications of rush and acceleration make us wonder whether high-speed society represents progress, or pathology. If the latter is the case we should simply slow down and arrest the illusory progress. We are already bombarded by diverse initiatives suggesting we should live more like a snail or tortoise. According to a website created by a prominent British journalist, James Harding, tortoises are slow, but wise, and so the message is: 'Slow down. Wise up.'[31] In this spirit slow food is recommended as a remedy for (unhealthy) fast food. Slow news is said to be better than (sensational) breaking news. Slow-paced legislative deliberation with numerous brakes on the executive is seen as a remedy for quick populist fixes. We are told to slow down economic development before we destroy the natural environment. Slowness rather than speed can even be more effective in war, some argue. Judicial deceleration is advocated to halt hyper-dramatized legal conflicts. The downshifting of personal life is suggested to avoid stress and the 'rat race'. We are urged to speak and think slowly because serious thoughts only function in a slow, systematic and reflective mode. Even slow sex and prayer are in vogue these days.

I am all in favour of slow food, prayer and sex, but I am aware that not everybody can afford slow food, while fast sex may be better than no sex. The judicial deceleration of the Italian court system, based upon my own experience, is not necessarily a good thing. Slowing down economic development has a different appeal in Switzerland than in Mozambique or Albania. Advocates of slow-paced legislative deliberation often have vested interests in maintaining the status quo and resisting any meaningful changes. In short, speeding up and slowing down have unequal implications for different groups of people and regions. For unemployed and homeless citizens or migrants, fashionable terms such as WFH or workcation have no sense whatsoever. These people have hardly experienced any acceleration in their life if one does not count efforts to provide food and shelter with no cash to spare. As William E. Connolly rightly observed, sometimes 'the crawl of slow time contains injuries, dangers and repressive tendencies'.[32] Speed, on the other hand, can have positive, and not only negative connotations. High speed can be chaotic and debilitating, but it can also be controlled and liberating. High speed can also save lives; think about emergency ambulances or the super-quick development of vaccines against Covid-19 (although the recent pandemic can itself be seen as a product of acceleration).

Moreover, notions of slowness and speed are relative and context-dependent. A driver of a sports car on an empty highway can drive much faster with no danger of a crash than a driver of a jeep on a very bumpy road. The former crosses a given distance in a much shorter period of time. The same logic applies to our political and economic institutions. As Ralf Dahrendorf observed in the context of Eastern European transitions three decades ago: 'It takes six months to create new political institutions, to write a constitution and electoral laws. It may take six years to create a half-way viable economy. It will probably take sixty years to create a civil society.'[33] A decade or so ago, during the Euro crisis, some southern Europeans discovered that it takes only a few hours to wipe out savings accumulated over many long years. Mariupol was levelled to the ground by the Russian shelling within two months. How much time will it take to rebuild this once vibrant city? Therefore, it is rather senseless to talk about choosing between high speed and deceleration, because there are fields where acceleration is badly required such as social housing, climate crisis, cancer prevention or post-war recovery. In fields such as law-making, road traffic or financial transactions, most of us can benefit from a certain deceleration. As Judy Wajcman observed: 'A fast/slow dichotomy cannot hope to capture the simultaneous coexistence of multiple temporalities that characterizes the experience of modernity.'[34]

Speeding up and slowing down is not always a matter of political choice because certain areas of our life are not particularly responsive to institutional engineering. All European governments have tried to accelerate economic growth, but most of them have failed to achieve much over the past five decades. Efforts to accelerate demographic growth have been equally futile in Europe, despite numerous incentives provided by states, such as maternity leave or cash payments for each newborn child. These failed attempts at acceleration led a famous social geographer, Danny Dorling, to put forward a forceful and well-evidenced argument suggesting that we are facing an overall slowdown rather than acceleration. 'Economically nearly everywhere is now slowing, especially in those places with the most people [including China]', wrote Dorling on the eve of the pandemic: 'We appear to be approaching a steady state economy similar to what ecologists call a steady state climatic climax community (think of a mature rain forest).'[35] This slowdown represents good news to Dorling because 'achieving greater economic stability, rather than simply accepting the roller coaster as usual, could help us bring about some [needed] changes more quickly and more carefully.'[36]

Standing still can hardly bring about needed change more quickly, given that in large parts of the Western world we are experiencing stagnation. If the argument is to move forward more slowly and more wisely, we need to explain how change can be generated.[37] After all, Dorling's impressive statistical graphs suggest that the slowdown we have experienced occurs by default rather than design. When I read books calling for economic stabilization rather than expansion, and for prosperity without growth, I have a feeling that we are simply trying to put a positive spin on our poor economic (or demographic) performance.[38]

Dorling does not negate the existence of the high-speed economy and society; in fact, he castigates it. This creates a fascinating paradox awaiting explanation. The period of overall slowdown coexists with the rise of the high-speed economy and society. If the latter is chiefly generated by technology, can the same technology represent a solution for improving our life in a stagnant economy and society? I have no sympathy for either techno-zealots or technophobes. I am more interested in figuring out how robotics and AI can be employed in the service of humanity without merely destroying jobs currently supporting numerous communities.[39] I am also interested in economic remedies that move us quickly forward without destroying our planet and leaving vast strata of society behind. Elinor Ostrom was one of the pioneers who showed how this could be accomplished by communities of individuals relying on institutions resembling neither the state nor the market.[40] Chris Benner and Manuel Pastor showed how, in the world of inequality, social divisions and ecological destruction, we could build economics based on cooperation rather than self-interest and greed.[41] We need vigorous rather than slow action to tackle economic insecurities and environmental destruction.[42]

Nostalgia for an idealized slow, allegedly natural, rhythm of work and life will not bring about tangible solutions for coping with the current problems related to the high speed of the economy and society. I am often in the Tuscan countryside surrounded by organic vineyards, and I see wine producers working 24/7 and selling their products online to numerous countries. This is why I am not convinced by Jeremy Rifkin's argument that one solution to high-speed society is organic farming, among others.[43] In 1980 I enjoyed watching the American comedy *9 to 5*, featuring Jane Fonda, Dolly Parton and Lily Tomlin.[44] But this does not mean that I insist on sticking to the 'nine to five' work schedule and oppose flexible working arrangements.

However, when moving to WFH or other forms of flexible labour, I want to make sure that employees' rights are being protected. I agree with Robert Goodin and his colleagues from the Australian National University that 'temporal autonomy' and 'discretionary time' represent a new 'measure of freedom'.[45] We can even go further and declare time a human right. As Robert Hassan argued, 'time is a resource, and should be considered in the same way as the right to freedom of speech or the protection against slavery'.[46] We claim ownership of space, and time should be treated in a similar way. We all have the right to enjoy time and share its benefits. When states dictate how long we are obliged to go to school, how many days we can enjoy free of work or when we should retire, they encroach on our right to shape the pace of our personal lives. Don't they?

How to uphold temporal autonomy and the right to free time is a matter of politics and law. We need to put time on the agenda, and press for solutions protecting our right to time. As argued earlier, time is man-made, and so it is up to us to shape its usage in a democratic way. While I accept that democratic deliberations should not be rushed, a prolonged indecision will hurt those of us who are part of high-speed capitalism and society. There is no time to waste!

5

MISMANAGED ROWDY SPACES

The 2007 film *Katyń*, directed by internationally acclaimed director Andrzej Wajda, starts at a bridge separating the areas of Soviet and German rule in Poland in 1940.[1] Crowds of confused and desperate Poles cross each other on this bridge, some fleeing German aggression, others Soviet. There seems to be no escape from one form of misery or another, and the border symbolized by the bridge affords them no protection whatsoever, no matter which direction they are heading. This opening of Wajda's film symbolizes the situation in which we find ourselves at present. We live in a very bordered world, but these borders offer little order, security or communal bonds. We may cross each other on the symbolic bridge, or even clash with each other on it, but we do not know whether reaching the other side amounts to any improvement. Even the extreme measure of blowing up the bridge seems futile, because we suspect that there is no safe place to hide. Admittedly, some of us are living in a state of denial, pretending that climate change, arms races and inequalities are not serious, at least for now. Yet I believe that most of us want to make the world a better place. The question is: how?

Erecting walls does not seem to be a plausible solution because walls instigate political and cultural conflicts instead of defusing them. However, a benign approach to borders stirs up public resistance because porous borders make it difficult to create communities willing to share their decisions and wealth. Governments have tried various solutions to the issue of borders, but they have usually amounted to a public relations exercise that pleased neither settlers nor nomads. Politics that are supposed to handle our interdependencies seem out of sync with developments on the ground. We struggle to understand this new space that is 'stretched, mobile and immaterial' to use Zygmunt Bauman's words.[2]

Sovereignty and power are becoming separated from the politics of the territorial nation-state, but are not being institutionalized in a new space. Uncertainty, randomness and indecisiveness are common – no matter who is in charge. The world resembles Jorge Luis Borges' lottery: a place where 'the number of drawings is infinite', 'no decision is final' and 'all branch into others'.[3]

Let's discuss spatial interdependencies in the most crucial fields of our life and see how they are managed or mismanaged. At the core of our discussion is the question of agency in governing global space. For the past few centuries, nation-states were the prime actors providing humans with security, welfare and a feeling of belonging. States are agents tied to a specific territory delimited by borders. When they try to address trans-border flows, they encroach on other states' borders and sovereignty. This chiefly explains why the state-based world system is not only conflict-ridden but dysfunctional when it comes to global problems. This is not to suggest that states are necessarily greedy and selfish. As I will try to show in the following sections, states have tried, but failed, to offer plausible governance in a world that is becoming progressively more interconnected.

Connectivity conflicts

For the past few decades, it was widely believed that conflicts can be defused by interaction, interdependence and interpenetration.[4] Interaction was practised through a vast array of international organizations and bilateral links – not just diplomatic but also military. NATO's Partnership for Peace is a good example of the latter. Even during the Cold War, a policy of détente was pursued, with the (Helsinki) Conference on Security and Cooperation in Europe as its main institutional vehicle. Interdependence was chiefly practised in the field of economics, guided by the principle that trade generates peace, because no rational actor is happy to jeopardize the profits stemming from trade. Interpenetration referred chiefly to rewarding mutual cultural influences, partly stemming from migration, and was seen as a factor defusing suspicion between potential enemies. As the eminent American professor Richard Rosecrance argued:

> Those who depended on others did better than those who depended only on themselves . . . Free movement of capital and goods, substantial international and domestic investment, and high levels of technical education have been the recipe for success in the industrialized world of the late twentieth century.[5]

All these assumptions are now being questioned to the extent that the leading international think-tank, the European Council on Foreign Relations, has published a book under the telling title *Connectivity Wars*.[6] Violence and war have continued despite ever-growing interdependence. In fact, some of the current conflicts are being generated by intense interaction, interpenetration and interdependence. Why is this so? Was it wrong to soften borders instead of hardening them? Will we feel safer behind walls?

First, we need to point out that borders have often been softened by default rather than by design. Nation-states never gave up control of their borders, even in the case of the EU: the selective opening of borders between member states went hand in hand with the hardening of the external EU border. In the heyday of economic globalization (2008–15), the big G20 countries added more than 1,200 restrictive export and import measures.[7] Participation in international peace-keeping operations never implied the abandonment of territorial defence (that is, defence of the territory of a given country). Territorial defence has been undermined by technological innovations in the military field, which allow 'enemies' to launch nuclear or cyberattacks with little regard for state borders.[8] Cultural 'wars' are now chiefly located on the internet, and states have limited ability to control them.

Politicians often instigate cultural wars; think of such leaders from the pre-social media era as Slobodan Milošević of Serbia, Omar al-Bashir of Sudan or Saddam Hussein of Iraq. However, more often than not, racism, nativism and religious fundamentalism are steered by cultural rather than political entrepreneurs, with clerics, poets and pop singers having their own distinct agendas. Zorica Brunclik, one of the best-known exponents of Serbia's populist folk music style, is a good example here.[9]

Second, interdependence may indeed defuse some conflicts, but it can also create new ones. Interdependence means that we are dependent on each other. Dependence means vulnerability and insecurity, because we cannot govern things single-handedly, the way we would like to. Of course, interdependence creates incentives to cooperate, but sometimes cooperation is difficult because we do not trust each other for historic reasons or because of asymmetries of power. In fact, states often exploit interdependency to strengthen their bargaining position. President Putin of Russia has used gas and oil supplies as a strategic weapon against energy-dependent states such as Ukraine, and in 2022 he extended this strategy to members of the European Union. President Erdoğan of Turkey has used Syrian refugees as a bargaining chip vis-à-vis the European Union. The EU, for its part, has made access to its market dependent on various political conditions. The ongoing US–China conflict largely stems from the countries' mutual interdependence.[10] Vulnerability to markets, religions and political ideologies crossing borders is also seen as a threat.

Third, interdependence does not do away with certain historic, violent conflicts. Ethnic conflicts are a good example here, and they tend to spread beyond national borders. Interdependence that concerns states does not extend to homogeneous (closed, insulated, contained) ethnic groups determined to defend their 'spiritual' territory: their homeland. Homeland has a cultural meaning, independent from economic or even strategic calculations. As my former colleague in Oxford, Monica Duffy Toft, explains:

> In many places of the world, borders and boundaries seem fixed in time and in the imagination. The name of the land has remained the same for generations, and the people inhabiting that land would rather die than lose the hope or right of return. In this context territory takes on a meaning that far exceeds its material and objective description. It becomes not an object to be exchanged but an indivisible component of a group's identity.[11]

Religious fundamentalism also ignores interdependence and the costs of conflict. Attacks on infidels are not guided by the quest for economic profits but by the desire to please God. After 9/11, our attention has been primarily focused on jihad, but intolerant and aggressive sects of believers can be found all over the world.[12]

The above observation explains why war is not obsolete despite (or even because of) heightened connectivity.[13] However, this does not mean that we should hurry to construct walls and bunkers to insulate ourselves from violence. The Poland of my childhood was separated from the Western 'enemy' by the wall running through divided Germany. The government was also building numerous bunkers to offer shelter against a projected nuclear attack, and as a child I practised emergency exercises with my school in those bunkers. The attack from the external enemy never took place, but the Polish authorities and their Soviet masters used the wall and war propaganda to spread the 'bunker mentality' and keep us obedient and passive. The détente policy advocated primarily by German Social Democrats envisaged limited economic interdependence, military interaction and societal interpenetration: the three famous 'baskets' of the Helsinki process. This policy proved fundamental to bringing down the wall and made my country free to choose its own path.[14] This newly acquired freedom has not always been used wisely by Poland's democratically elected politicians. New enemies have been invented – feminists, Jews, refugees and the LGBT+ community. No wonder the topic of walls and ghettos is returning to Poland's political agenda, especially on the web. The Russian invasion of Poland's neighbour has only further reinforced the 'bunker mentality' in Poland.

This personal vignette suggests that walls and bunkers do not necessarily create security and prevent conflicts. The key question is whether we live in an open or closed society. A closed society sees interdependence as a threat, and tries to manipulate trade, international organizations and cultural exchanges to its own parochial advantage. An open society sees interdependence as an opportunity, and tries to create institutions that reduce mutual suspicion, mitigate inequalities and prevent free riding. A closed society sees international politics as a zero-sum game in which stronger actors can enjoy territorial sovereignty, while the weaker ones are forced to keep their borders open to 'alien' soldiers, goods and ideologies. An open society tries to share sovereignty and to use open borders for mutual advantage through the diffusion of knowledge and best practices. The problem is that the distinction between open and closed societies is often blurred. Despite President Trump's campaign to seal the borders and to frustrate international cooperation, the United States of America remained an open society to a large extent. Politicians often betray noble policy goals in their daily practice. The Labour government of Tony Blair initially promised an 'ethical foreign policy', but ended with the cruel invasion of Iraq.[15] Most crucially in our spatial context, the institutional guardians of open society – constitutions, parliaments and public broadcasters – are linked to the territory of nation-states, and not to international institutions that are supposed to handle interdependence. And it is difficult to argue against efforts to reinforce borders when we are threatened by aggression from a mighty neighbour.

In today's world, it may at times be hard to understand why people are prepared to die defending a certain piece of land. However, if we believe that an open society is the surest way to prevent war and violence, we need to locate this society on a land or space where the institutions of an open society can thrive. This is why some of us believe that only nation-states can secure peace, even though this belief is not grounded in historical evidence. Some states are even responsible for the gravest atrocities in human history. The problem is that institutions of the open society, like flowers, are not likely to blossom on shifting sands. Can we envisage a well-functioning open society in an unbounded space?

Trans-border economics

The organization and management of space proves particularly tricky in the field of economics. The globalization of production, markets, finance, technology, corporations and labour is often blamed for the pathologies of present-day capitalism such as unprecedented inequalities, capital flight undercutting social provisions and labour, the mismanagement of natural resources causing ecological damage, dependence on fragile supply chains, 'McDonaldization' and tax havens. The question of who is responsible for screwing up globalization is a pertinent one. How come the project that was supposed to promote global economic growth, create jobs, lower consumer prices, make companies more competitive, and spread liberal ideals is now blamed for causing multiple crises and injustice? Ironically, one of the few countries still fond of globalization is now China, run by the heirs of the ultra-autarchic Chairman Mao.[16]

Unlike in the field of security, where nation-states are seen as prime actors, in the field of economics the finger is usually pointed at private firms, especially huge multinationals. The predatory behaviour of some of these firms has been particularly exposed in the aftermath of the 2008–10 financial crisis.[17] However, there is also an important body of literature which does not absolve states from the responsibility for mismanaging the global economy. Joseph Stiglitz, who won the Nobel Prize for Economics in 2001, argued that 'the advanced industrial countries actually created a global trade regime that helped their special corporate and financial interests, and hurt the poorest countries of the world'.[18] Advanced industrial states, according to Stiglitz, not only failed to do 'all that they could to help' poor countries through the International Monetary Fund (IMF), the World Trade Organization (WTO) and the World Bank, but were sometimes making life in poor countries 'more difficult'.[19] (We should keep in mind that these international bodies are controlled by the advanced industrialized states.)

We now know that economic globalization was a double-edged sword, and so the policies orchestrated by advanced industrialized countries began to hurt those who promoted them. For instance, according to estimates by Robert Scott of the Economic Policy Institute, granting China 'most favoured nation' status drained away 3.2 million American jobs, including 2.4 million manufacturing jobs.[20] Donald Trump was elected US President on the promise of reversing globalization by repudiating existing trade agreements, slapping taxes on US companies investing overseas, establishing tariffs to discourage companies from off-shoring production as well as jobs, and building a wall to keep economic migrants out of the country.[21] Failure to 'save the welfare state by making it fit for a global economy' has also been lamented by the enemies of Trump on the left of the political spectrum in Europe and the United States.[22]

It would be a mistake to focus merely on individual regulatory decisions or trade agreements in trying to explain states' failure to manage the global economic space. As Philip Bobbitt, a renowned American scholar has documented, the nation-state after 1990 has undergone an important conversion; it has transformed itself into the market-state.[23] The sovereignty of the nation-state was linked to its territorial borders. However, with the spread of universal (regional and global) laws, economic exchanges and communication, the nature and the purpose of the state has changed. The market-state does not see its role as the key provider of economic services and goods, Bobbitt argues. Instead of economic redistribution, it is interested in maximizing opportunities for all groups of citizens. The national currency is one among many commodities for this new form of state, and full employment is not paramount to its economic strategy. In its global policy, the market-state is more interested in making the world safe for business than for democracy. 'Universalizing opportunity' is part of this global agenda and so is greater 'transparency and citizen participation', however symbolic. (Bobbitt believes that 'there will be more public participation in government, but it will count for less'.)[24] Although traditional domestic social programmes will be curtailed, the market-state, according to Bobbitt, will put greater emphasis on infrastructure security, epidemiological surveillance and environmental protection. Since the latter require regional and global provisions, this would represent an important step towards the internationalization of matters of general welfare.

Bobbitt's analysis has important implications for understanding the process of economic globalization. It suggests that economic actors have not escaped the (democratic) controls of the state by moving their transactions beyond state borders; rather, they have advanced transnational transactions with the support of their (market) states. Thus if we want to eradicate the pathologies of globalized economics we need to reform not just markets but also states because states are as responsible for these pathologies as are markets. We should keep this in mind in the post-Covid-19 era, which is largely about bringing states back in.[25] Bringing (unreformed) states back into the process of economic decision-making may prove futile, if not counter-productive.[26] Since states cannot be reformed overnight, we need to think about alternative paths. Perhaps we should bring back other public actors such as cities or regions and empower international actors, not just those controlled by states, but also those rooted in civil society.

Firms and states do not act in an ideological vacuum. We may now feel like we are living in 'an open sea', captured well by Bauman, but prior to the 2008 financial crash we seemed to know exactly what economic success required: minimal regulation, low taxes and powerless trade unions.[27] The privatization or marketization of public services such as energy, water, railways, health, education, roads and prisons was also widely acclaimed. Even waging war and promoting homeland security was privatized.[28] The state was supposed to help failing banks and inefficient car factories, but not the unemployed or those living on the state pension. Anybody who questioned free choice, free competition and the free market would be called irrational and irresponsible, if not stupid. This dominant neoliberal ideology is largely responsible for entrenched inequalities, the erosion of the public sector, financial meltdowns and widespread ecological damage. Open borders were part of the neoliberal agenda, which explains why the critics of neoliberalism from the political Left and Right demand the hardening of borders. However, the situation would probably be different today had various transnational flaws been subject to public oversight, extensive regulation and sound mechanisms of redistribution. The sovereigntists criticizing transnational flows are simply barking up the wrong tree. Inequalities were generated by neoliberal policies that put markets in charge of redistribution. They are also the result of a belief system in which competitiveness is more cherished than solidarity. Open borders have little to do with either of these.

Competition between the most powerful states also perverted the nature of global economic exchanges. As Helen Thompson from the University of Cambridge wrote in the *New Statesman*:

> For two decades, cheap labour in China drove consumer prices down. But when goods are produced in a world of fear and geopolitical rivalry, their origins, not just their cost, really matter. [Trump] reoriented the US towards open technological competition with Beijing, and told the EU and Britain they would have to adjust towards this strategic rivalry or face the consequences for NATO.[29]

It should be kept in mind, however, that major protagonists in this global geopolitical battle – the United States, China, the European Union and Russia – all have imperial characteristics that are distinct from those of traditional nation-states, especially in spatial terms.[30] They all represent huge territorial units with sizeable power resources, enabling them to influence, if not manipulate, domestic politics beyond their respective borders. They all claim that their values and norms are not just noble, but also universal. Since 'average' nation-states are unable to back their global economic expansion with the military hardware and cultural appeal available to empires, we can hardly talk about equal and fair global economic competition. So, if we want to make globalization work, we need to change not only the modes of investment, production, redistribution and trade, but also the nature of power politics.

The barbarians are at the door

Migration is one of the hottest political topics related to the management of global space. Politicians such as Viktor Orbán of Hungary or Matteo Salvini of Italy suggest that 'human traffickers' are the key actors responsible for migration, with NGOs helping migrants increasingly being blamed as well. Yet migration is not orchestrated by NGOs and traffickers; it is primarily caused by war and poverty – for which a great chunk of responsibility must be attributed to states. For instance, according to official UN data, the ongoing war in Syria has forced 6.6 million Syrians to flee their country, and I have already mentioned the millions fleeing the Russian assault on Ukraine.[31]

Of course, the war in Syria has many 'fathers', President Bashar al-Assad the most prominent among them. Yet the confusing policies towards Syria by democratic states such as France, the United Kingdom and the United States have not made things any better. In fact, the case of Syria shows that both external intervention and non-intervention may have damaging effects.[32] The cases of Afghanistan, Yugoslavia, Iraq, Sudan, Ukraine and Libya show a similar linkage between war, foreign intervention and migration.[33] In each of these cases, the legitimacy and the wisdom of foreign interventions can be debated, but the stimulus for migration was always beyond doubt.

Not only foreign, but also the domestic policies of states explain why migration is seen as poorly managed by states. The liberal policy of multiculturalism has come under fire, especially in the context of 'failed' Muslim integration in respective (Western) societies. In some countries, governments have been criticized for not sufficiently intervening to make 'illiberal' minorities adopt local values, while in other countries governments have been criticized for not 'fortifying' local national cultures and letting them dissipate under the pressure of 'privileged' ethnic minorities.[34]

The economic policies of states have also been blamed for not properly addressing migration. Exploitative 'post-colonial' policies are said to continue to cause poverty and brain drain in various parts of the world, including Europe. Investment in countries generating migrants has often been scarce, and half-hearted aid policies have treated surface-level poverty only.[35] While states, under corporate pressure, might have been eager to attract foreign migrants, they have done little to protect the local population from overcrowded hospitals and schools caused by the influx of migrant workers. Since migrants were often well-trained and demanded lower pay than local employees, conflicts between the foreign and local labour force flourished, fuelling xenophobic politics.

The United Kingdom is a good example here. After the 2004 EU enlargement, Great Britain decided to instantly welcome Eastern Europeans to fill the gaps in the labour market and stimulate economic growth.[36] The number of EU workers in the UK subsequently increased from 2.6 per cent to 6.8 per cent over a decade, most of them coming from Poland and other new EU member states. This influx of labour clearly helped Britain to get out of the recession and also created extra jobs for British citizens.[37] Yet those places with the highest concentration of new foreign labour experienced a 'culture shock' and new pressures on local services were neglected by the government. Instead of admitting its mistakes, the government began to blame the EU for the influx of foreign labour, and immigrant workers for exploiting the British social welfare system. The latter claim was never backed by any evidence. Her Majesty's Revenue and Customs (HMRC) figures show that migrants who arrived in Britain from the EU since 2011 have paid £2.5 billion more in tax and national insurance than they received in tax credits and social benefits. However, the Pandora's box had been opened. Anti-immigration feelings became widespread, leading to a surge in support for the 'yes' vote in the Brexit referendum. A good (visceral) example of this is the Lincolnshire town of Boston, where there are very high numbers of Eastern European immigrants, Polish stores on the high street, and votes for Brexit were the highest in the country.[38]

Governments tend to use public pressure against migration to justify the introduction of stringent, inhumane and often unlawful border security measures, but there is ample evidence suggesting that citizens are more upset by the shambolic migration policies of their governments than by the influx of migrants. Data consistently show that migrants contribute to the economic development of receiving states and most observe local laws and cultures.[39] Moreover, as the extensive empirical evidence offered by Professor Nick Vaughan-Williams shows, anti-migrant narratives usually originate at the top rather than bottom of societal ladders, aggravating anxieties among ordinary citizens.[40] Vaughan-Williams points to the counter-narrative whereby citizens in the receiving countries are more open and hospitable vis-à-vis migrants than is usually assumed and are not inclined to erect walls and new borders, which most people find ineffective anyway. Bashing Polish and Romanian migrants, among others, has cost the UK free access to the EU single market, and caused labour shortages. Bashing all Islamists indiscriminately implies that extremists were given shelter among the ordinary Muslim citizens of Holland, Belgium, France and Germany. Denying the value of multi-culturalism in the United States of America, Canada and Australia is an affront to generations of migrants who made these countries secure and prosperous.[41]

Migration is part of human history and all efforts to stop it completely have failed. However, we can handle migration effectively and ethically.[42] Providing routes for legal migration and work visas can actually promote legal migration and circular migration, where people eventually return to their country of origin (for example, as in the case of Mexico and the United States), often bringing financial wealth, new entrepreneurial skills and cultural inputs.[43] The idea floated by some politicians that in order to stop 'barbarians' you need to act in a barbaric way is self-defeating. Governments targeting migrants are often eager to persecute different minority groups residing within their borders. In Hungary and Poland, governmental campaigns against refugees have been followed by campaigns against Jews, feminists, LGBT+ people and even environmentalists. Effective migration policies are not about building new walls, but about foreign and economic policies that reduce inequalities between the affluent and poor parts of the world. Above all, effective migration policies require peace and stability that can hardly be obtained by shady deals with dictators promising to keep migrants within their borders. Therefore, the EU deal with President Erdoğan to keep migrants in detention camps on Turkish territory has rightly been criticized as neither ethical nor effective in the long run. Similar arrangements are being orchestrated in states neighbouring Afghanistan following the US and European withdrawal there and the subsequent refugee flow.[44] Rwanda has witnessed some of the greatest atrocities in recent decades, and yet in 2022 the UK government signed a Memorandum of Understanding with Rwanda to send asylum seekers to the east African country, where their asylum claims will be processed. 'Experience shows that these agreements are eye-wateringly expensive', said Larry Bottinick, a senior legal officer for the UN High Commissioner

for Refugees. 'They often violate international law. They don't lead to solutions, rather to widespread detention or to more smuggling.'[45]

An effective migration policy also requires a domestic political battle. Politicians ought to have practical solutions for coping with migration and the courage to face their respective electorates. National politicians are not well-suited to engage in genuine dialogue with the public about migration because they treat state borders as sacred. In contrast, large cities are usually multi-ethnic with a different conception of space, ethnicity and authority. Residence permits rather than passports are crucial in cities. Instead of designing naturalization tests checking migrants' allegiance to a given national culture, municipal politicians prefer to focus on the practical matters confronting migrants such as housing, jobs, health, schools and security on the streets. There are various ways of treating migrants with respect that do not envisage relinquishing control of laws and borders as alleged by xenophobic politicians. Scaremongering is not a synonym for political dialogue.

The long history of migration has taught us a few simple lessons. There is no such thing as splendid isolation. Nor are there magic bullets to reduce migration. It is easier to construct walls than to tame wars or eradicate poverty in the less developed countries. However, walls are counter-productive because they help those in power to control 'hosts' rather than 'guests'. Migration is a challenge and an opportunity; much depends on how it is handled or, if you wish, governed. Compassion and morality do not need to end at the border. We are all humans in the end, no matter where we come from and where we live.

Climate unbound

Migration will be increasingly fuelled by climate change. Yet it is hard to deny that climate governance has failed miserably. Governments have signed numerous international agreements and made countless pledges to reduce emissions of greenhouse gases, and yet human-induced (anthropogenic) climate change has not been arrested or even slowed, but proceeds apace. The 2021 report issued by the Intergovernmental Panel on Climate Change (IPCC) made things painfully clear: 'Climate change [is] widespread, rapid and intensifying.'[46] We are doing too little and too late, which means that unstoppable climate impacts will soon be triggered with dire implications for many of us, and even more so for our children. These implications will be felt in all previously discussed areas: security, economics and migration.

Why is this so? A few decades ago, public perceptions of climate change and the related dangers were still limited, while scientists struggled to identify workable solutions to address global environmental problems. Today, environmental campaigners such as Greta Thunberg are known even in the most remote places of the world, and it is hard to keep count of the new books telling us how to make climate policy work and how to save our planet.[47] Even populist parties such as the Rassemblement National in France now have climate change policies on their manifestos. Corporate giants such as Microsoft have set the agenda to go carbon negative by 2030, while Unilever and Coca-Cola have teamed up with the leading environmental NGO, Greenpeace. In the United Kingdom a leading restaurant chain has promised 'carbon-neutral' burgers and fries, while BP, the leading global 'polluter', declared its ambition to be a 'net zero company'.[48] It looks like the buck stops with you and me, ordinary citizens. Without dramatic changes to our eating, heating or commuting habits it is hard to halt ongoing climate change.

There is no doubt that changing our long-standing habits can contribute to slowing climate change. For instance, switching from a standard Western meat-based diet to a vegetarian diet will halve our dietary greenhouse gas emissions, while switching from a personal car to public transport can reduce our household carbon footprint by up to 30 per cent.[49] Yet governments and firms too easily point fingers at individuals rather than themselves. This is not only because Saudi Aramco, Chevron, National Iranian Oil, Coal India, PetroChina or Gazprom made huge profits by destroying our atmosphere with the 'blessing' and protection of their respective states.[50] It is also if not chiefly because stopping climate change requires orchestrated collective efforts that steer societies towards environmentally sustainable outcomes. Governments, communities, industries and individuals must work together across time and space. This is the essence of climate change governance, which has so far manifested 'chronic and pathological failure', to use Paul G. Harris' words.[51]

We lack mechanisms that would effectively bridge the gap between those who profit from polluting and those who suffer

from environmental degradation. How can small islands on the frontline of climatic impacts make polluting mega-firms and states change their course dramatically? How to align the interests of energy-importing India with energy-exporting Saudi Arabia? How to bridge environmental threat perceptions between the older generation holding power, and the younger generation with no political levers? How can we stop using coal when faced with energy shortages orchestrated by Russia?

Moreover, there is no mechanism to bridge the political, institutional and economic domains of climate change governance. These domains or theatres take up different spaces, feature different actors, require different time perspectives, and work according to different logics. So far, the policies evolving in each of these fields undermine rather than support the others. For instance, the prime objective in the political theatre is power, in the economic domain the objective is profit, while the institutional objective in the environmental field is survival. The economic theatre is regional and global, while the political theatre is chiefly confined to national borders where elections are held. The institutional theatre is controlled by nation-states, subject to global economic trends, and dependent on the local implementation of decisions. Each of these theatres follows a different time schedule. Markets value instant revenue, the electoral cycle of politicians is usually four years, and climate change institutions must deliver change measured in decades. There is no mechanism that would bring these different time schedules into harmony and, by the same token, generate policies able to arrest if not reverse climate change.

The story of the 2016 Paris Agreement on Climate Change shows well how the disjuncture between these three theatres results in a kind of organized hypocrisy, or plain 'fraud' to use the words of James Hansen, the former NASA scientist considered the father of global awareness of climate change.[52] After several years of protracted negotiations led by states, facilitated by international institutions, and informed by economic firms, we formally have a legally binding international treaty on climate change, adopted by nearly 200 states. Yet if you study this document carefully, you find numerous vague aims and assurances but hardly any firm commitments. 'We'll have a 2C warming target and then try to do a little better every five years' – observed Hansen – 'It's just worthless words. There is no action, just promises. As long as fossil fuels appear to be the cheapest fuels out there, they will continue to be burned.'[53] In fact, five years after signing the Agreement, most states are still not on track to meeting its goals.[54] The second largest global polluter and the key negotiator in Paris, the United States, has been boycotting the Agreement practically from the start, formally withdrew from it in 2020, and re-joined in 2021 following the change of guard at the White House. Turkey and Iran have not even ratified the Paris Agreement. China is a signatory, but it continues to be the world's pollution champion, generating 30 per cent of all global carbon emissions. The 2021 COP26 world climate summit in Glasgow has even managed to 'water down the blah, blah, blah' language of previous agreements, concluded Greta Thunberg.[55] Clearly, the call of civic activists who gathered in Glasgow to 'end climate betrayal' has not been heard by state leaders.[56]

Arresting climate change requires the determined, coordinated action of numerous actors, yet the instruments to orchestrate such an action are chiefly in the hands of nation-states. States control major international institutions, they have the monopoly to issue laws binding citizens and corporations, and they also have at their disposal an array of economic incentives and sanctions, taxes most prominent among them. Corporations would not be able to sabotage global efforts to combat climate change if brought to justice by states. Citizens would make different consumer choices if states created appropriate incentives and sanctioned misbehaviour. States can lay the foundations for a circular economy, extracting energy from the environment and using tax revenues to support communities reliant on carbon-producing industries and agriculture to survive climate-induced changes. Yet states are more interested in defending their sovereignty and abstract national interest than in responding collectively to the climate change emergency. Environmental campaigners and whistle-blowers are ignored if not harassed by states. Tax systems often reward environmental predators rather than those applying renewable energy. In fact, states around the world still spend US $5 trillion on subsidizing fossil fuels! Successive global summits on climate change have become arenas of national competition producing vague commitments and fake progress. As the former German politician Joschka Fischer states:

> The central conundrum of the climate crisis is that we must rely on the structures of a global system based on the egoism of nation-states. Joint action to fend off a common threat on behalf of all humanity must be taken through the narrower, older channels of sovereignty. The idea of global responsibility to maintain the basis for our common survival is alien to such a system. Coming to grips with this disconnect will be the great challenge of the twenty-first century.[57]

Fischer's pointing at states and the global state-system should surprise nobody. We have found states to be the chief protagonists or even culprits in generating wars, mismanaging the global economy and mishandling migration. Why is this so? Why do we continue to rely on states to govern our globe?

Redefining public authority

The system of states is not an 'accident' of history. For the past few centuries, nation-states were the prime governing agencies. They prevailed over medieval kingdoms, cities, principalities and even Papacy and Empire because they were able to exercise authority over diverse economic, administrative, military and cultural borders.[58] Most notably, they managed to provide an overlap between these borders and construct a centralized rule within them.

States governed their spaces with a mixture of hierarchy and responsiveness. Democracies have obviously envisaged more of the latter, while autocracies the former. The inter-state system has been much more 'anarchic', kept in check by various forms of hegemony and diplomacy. States are still around, despite repeated gloomy predictions of their decay, and some of them are still able to maintain relative order in their respective peripheries. Nationalism, one of the key pillars sustaining states, is as alive as ever. However, new technologies, changing patterns of economic engagements, cultural diversi-fication, and novel forms of communication have transformed states and the system of states beyond recognition. Most crucially in our context, states are no longer able to provide an overlap between administrative boundaries, military frontiers, cultural traits and economic fringes. This flips the system of governance led by states on its head, leaving citizens in limbo in various fields and places. What is the value of the state if it cannot protect citizens from extra-territorial legal claims, transnational financial speculations or devastating climate change? Why should citizens rally under national flags if their nation-states chiefly enrich the famous or infamous 1 per cent? Are states generating security, or insecurity? The challenge is to regain public control over the rowdy spaces that generate inequalities, conflicts and feelings of helplessness. The key questions are: with what, and how?

The question 'with what' is relatively easy to answer. States should play an important role in governing space, but they should not have a monopoly on decision-making and resources. Other public actors such as regions and cities should play a greater role, as well as a plethora of private actors, starting with firms and NGOs. International organizations such as the United Nations, European Union or NATO can also perform better if freed from the veto powers of member states. Instead of top-down governance led by states, we need diversified networks of partnership and cooperation. This can be done in various ways, depending on the regional or functional context. For instance, the EU could create a second chamber of the European Parliament featuring these non-state actors. We should also acknowledge the importance of informal networks, and make them work within commonly agreed laws. And we should make sure that states do not abuse patriotic feelings for the benefit of a small national circle in power. Jan-Werner Müller from Princeton University put it well: 'Globalization has not brought the end of nationalism but opportunities to retreat selectively from society.'[59]

The question of 'how' is trickier because much depends on the nature of the spatial issues to be tackled. Migration, security and climate change are interlinked, but they require different governing solutions. One thing is certain: governance ought to be effective and responsive. You cannot separate one from another. Responsiveness without efficiency results in frustration and even anarchy in some cases. Effectiveness without responsiveness results in autocracy.[60] Yet neither effectiveness nor responsiveness is possible without a common public sense

of direction on how to govern our space: local and global, territorial and digital, terrestrial and outer space. If some of us
believe that unbounding represents a solution to our problems,
we need to reach a compromise with those preferring
re-bounding. This is why democracy, with its procedures to
manage conflicting positions, is important. But if democracy is
'up in the air', unable to relate to any space or people inhabiting the space, then we've got a problem.

While it is evident that democracy within many states has degenerated, sound alternatives at either the regional or global level have not emerged. The notion of cosmopolitan democracy is still a myth, while democracy within the EU is being manipulated by member states. This does not mean that democracy is doomed, because a variety of civic institutions and the independent media monitor those in power and pressure them to comply with laws and moral norms. However, we need to go further and embrace democratic experiments that can make states and various transnational networks accountable to citizens. Paradoxically, governing an ever-larger space would require strengthening citizens' participation at the local level. As the leading democratic theorist, Robert A. Dahl, argued: 'The larger scale of decisions need not lead inevitably to a widening sense of powerlessness, provided citizens can exercise significant control over decisions on the smaller scale of matters important to their daily lives: education, public health, town and city planning.'[61] I will try to envisage the democratic governance of transnational networks in Chapter 7. But for now let me only say that networks are not mysterious floating islands contributing to our confusion. Networks have always been part of our governance, and have proved better-suited to handling interdependence than formal hierarchical structures such as nation-states. To paraphrase the great Czech writer, Milan Kundera, good governing, like good writing, requires 'breaking through a wall behind which something immutable ("the poem") lies hidden in darkness'.[62]

6

POLITICAL PAST AND FUTURE

On 12 July 2021, Russia's President Putin published a long article entitled 'On the Historical Unity of Russians and Ukrainians'.[1] The article 'analysed' this region's history over more than one thousand years to show that 'the idea of Ukrainian people as a nation separate from the Russians started to form and gain ground among the Polish elite and a part of the Malorussian [Little Russian] intelligentsia' in the nineteenth century and it was subsequently 'used for political purposes as a tool of rivalry between European states'. He also blamed the father of the Soviet Union, Lenin, and his successors for tolerating the 'myth' of Ukrainian independence. When the Soviet Union collapsed, Ukraine's ruling circles decided to justify their country's independence through the denial of its past, according to Putin; they began to 'mythologize and rewrite history, edit out everything that united Ukraine and Russia'.

Independent historians, such as Victoria Smolkin, called Putin's analysis 'fantasy, not history' that leaves out important facts related to Ukrainian nation- and state-building.[2] However, less than eight months after the publication of Putin's bizarre historical tirade, Russia embarked on the full-scale invasion of Ukraine with the supposed aim of securing a bright future for the united Russian and Ukrainian people. In his televised address on the eve of the invasion, Putin repeated most of the historical arguments from the article cited above and concluded that Ukraine's claim to statehood was entirely baseless because the country was an integral part of Russia's 'own history, culture, spiritual space'.[3]

The past is politicians' favourite solution for addressing the future; and not just to justify future invasions, as was the case with Putin. The past is used to divert citizens from all kinds of problems facing countries and their people. When politicians have little reassurance to offer about the clouds gathering over our heads, they talk about heroic or glorious history. In the midst of the Covid-19 pandemic, President Trump repeatedly defended monuments in honour of Confederate figures, while ignoring the recommendations of his own coronavirus team to arrest the spread of the virus.[4] The post-Brexit future has been framed by the Tory government as a return to imperial grandeur, with little regard for the practical and legal implications of leaving the EU.[5] In 2022, while the country grappled with the worst cost of living crisis in decades, Johnson's government hyped up the Platinum Jubilee and suggested reintroducing the imperial weight measures of pounds and ounces for the sake of nostalgia. In Poland, the people in charge of this leading European polluter have done little to get rid of coal mines, but have spent an enormous amount of time and energy in order to give Poland's history a 'facelift'. Shameful historical episodes such as the denunciation and killing of Jews in the 1940s have been downplayed, or denied altogether, and new national heroes have been created and celebrated.

To address the future, you need a strategy and resources, but to address the past you only need rhetorical skills. You do not even need to know history to talk about the past. The past can be tailored to suit the demands of those in power with the help of friendly media and politically appointed heads of museums and institutes of national memory. New monuments can be installed, names of streets and squares can be changed, and teaching curricula can be revised. Rewriting and reinventing history does not require huge budgets, and it chiefly offends people who are already long dead.

In the midst of a financial or health crisis, voters may feel reassured by historical examples of battles won, economic miracles and moral purity. Questioning these historic myths may deprive citizens of the hope that is needed in difficult periods. This is why politicians never tire of urging us to look on the bright side and to be proud of our past. Dark chapters in our history evoke gloom and feelings of hopelessness, while what we need is optimism. In some states, you can even go to jail for undermining past achievements and, by the same token, allowing 'enemies' to exploit historical wrongdoings. After Russia's president declared that the 'excessive demonization' of Stalin has been a 'means of attacking the Soviet Union and Russia', the authorities cracked down on institutions revealing Stalin's crimes, such as the well-known human rights group, Memorial.[6]

Addressing the future is a thorny challenge for politicians. Environmental policies require huge budgets, as do pension reforms and public infrastructure projects aimed at renovating roads, schools and hospitals. Reaching into voters' pockets to cover these costs is seldom popular. Facing off the resistance of those who benefit from the status quo requires bribes that governments cannot afford. Besides, it is quite awkward for politicians to antagonize financial donors to their parties, who want to keep things as they are. And there is also a problem with evidencing the possible returns of all these future-oriented investments. Does it make sense to embark on costly policies that may (or may not) result in improvements enjoyed by future generations of voters and politicians? When it comes to the future, nothing is one hundred per cent certain, despite all our scientific advances.[7] This uncertainty is compounded in periods of ideological confusion when we no longer know what is good and evil, how to distinguish truth from post-truth, and where the border lies between normality and absurdity.

Talking about the good old days is more comforting than talking about the messy future.[8] It is easier to handle resistance to renaming a city square than to imposing carbon emission taxes affecting the drivers of diesel vehicles, for instance. A new museum costs less than a new hospital, and you need more than one hospital to enjoy a popularity boost. Besides, a museum speaks to politicians' rank and file, while most future threats are transnational in nature and require transnational solutions. Can democracy acting on behalf of a national *demos* handle problems that are regional or global in their nature? We talk about history in our respective national languages, not in some kind of Esperanto required to address our collective future.

Let's reflect on how the past is used and misused to shape the future. This discussion is not just about political PR, but also, if not chiefly, about the temporal horizons of modern democracy. In a high-speed era, democracy is ever more concerned with short-term rather than long-term fears and hopes. This is the major focus of this chapter. We start with history, because history may be the ideal guide to march through life with a perspective that is not obsessed with the present. History may also help us to avoid repeating mistakes of the past in the future. Unfortunately, in the world of politics, focusing on history is often intended to divert our attention from the future and present. And I will argue that politically manufactured history is a poor guide for any traveller. However, citizens may also be more interested in focusing on the past rather than the future, and they tend to idealize the past in the same way as politicians. Some of us are afraid of change and prefer to cultivate myths about the cosy if not glorious past. Others are simply resisting change because they want to maintain a status quo from which they draw various sorts of privileges. Politicians may well exploit our fears and manufacture historical myths for justifying current and future policies. However, nostalgic politics thrives in an environment of historical resentments, nationalistic ambitions and post-truth. To use economic jargon: it is hard to sell historical 'products' for which there is no public demand.

Before we conclude that our selfish populist instincts prevent future-oriented policies, let me suggest a different argument. Perhaps our resistance to embracing change for the benefit of the future stems from democratic deficiencies. If we do not trust democracy to deliver the expected results, we are unlikely to endorse forward-facing projects, especially expensive ones. True, some politicians may well be incompetent if not corrupt, but trust in governments to live up to their promises seems low even in affluent and relatively well functioning European states. When asked on the eve of the 2022 presidential elections whether the French political system worked or was broken, 69 per cent of French respondents said it was either completely or somewhat broken.[9] Is it wise to put faith in a broken political system promising to secure the future?

The politics of history

We used to joke in Communist Poland that the future is certain, but the past is constantly changing. The future was secure in the Party's hands, we were told, but the history in people's memories did not match the one in newspapers and textbooks. The Americans who came to rescue Europe from Hitler were now the enemies, and the Russians who invaded Poland jointly with Hitler were now our friends. (The eastern part of Poland was invaded by Soviet troops in September 1939 as stipulated in the secret Molotov-Ribbentrop Pact.) After 1989, this history was reversed. Monuments in tribute to Soviet 'friends' were destroyed, and the Americans became Poland's greatest friends. There is now a monument to Ronald Reagan in Warsaw, and a large square next to my old flat was renamed Woodrow Wilson Square. (In another example of the changing past, Wilson's legacy is now under attack in the United States. In June 2020, the Princeton University Board of Trustees concluded that Woodrow Wilson's racist thinking and policies make him an inappropriate namesake for a school or college whose scholars, students and alumni must stand firmly against racism in all its forms.)

The toppling of monuments in 2020 related to the Black Lives Matter movement came as a surprise to many of the British and Americans. However, in other parts of the world this is a familiar practice marking a break in perceptions of the past and the longing for a new beginning. In Ukraine, since the beginning of the Euromaidan protests in 2013, over 900 Lenin monuments have been removed as the country turned definitively away from its Communist past and Russian influence.[10] Statues of Saddam Hussein were toppled across Iraq after his defeat in the war of 2003. After the fall of the Third Reich in 1945, monuments raised by the Nazi regime were knocked down across Germany and beyond. In Revolutionary France, sculptures of kings were even guillotined. Recently in Belgium, statues of King Leopold II, who is held responsible for various atrocities in pre-First World War Congo, have been defaced, painted in (bloody) red or graffitied with words like 'murderer'.[11]

The conflict over monuments is not just symbolic, and its gravity should not be underestimated. In the midst of the battle over contested monuments in the United States (22 June 2020), a Rasmussen poll found that 34 per cent of Americans felt that a civil war was likely within five years.[12] The historic figures on our monuments represent a set of values that we admire or detest. Lenin and Stalin may be unpopular in Ukraine or Lithuania, but they are enjoying a renaissance in Russia, not just among leaders, but also among ordinary Russian citizens who long for their country's imperial glory, however illusory. President Putin's decision to invade Ukraine illustrates the practical implications of this misguided imperial nostalgia. 'The imperial table can once again be reset', wrote Ivan Krastev in this context. 'These people [Russian security officials] are not interested in writing the future, they want to rewrite the past.'[13]

Treatment of monuments is not just about the past, but also about the future and present. Those who defend statues of Churchill, Cromwell and even Colston cherish a different vision of the United Kingdom than those who contest these statues. The former are fond of tradition, authority and empire, while the latter are more interested in freedom, equality and racial justice.

Monuments are not only about specific symbolic persons, but also about the kind of society we value and celebrate. A recent study by Art UK examining London's 1,500 statues and sculptures found that 79 per cent of named figures are men.[14] Only 4 per cent of public statues represent women, while 8 per cent depict animals. People of colour make up a mere 1 per cent of statues; and a tiny 0.2 per cent are women of colour. The most frequently depicted woman is Queen Victoria, the nineteenth-century symbol of British imperial grandeur. No wonder the progressive Mayor of London concluded that statues in his city are in dire need of an equality and diversity shake-up, and launched a special commission aimed at projecting a different kind of urban society than is the case at present.[15]

We can have a sensible conversation about the specific historical record of people featuring on monuments, but as a famous historian from Cambridge argued, monuments are not about history, but about memory, and we should not confuse the two: 'Awarding ticks and crosses to the people of the past, canonising some as heroes and damning others as villains' is not history, argues Richard J. Evans.[16] History is an academic discipline teaching us how to collect and interpret documents. It is not about moralising specific episodes from the past, and dictating the only 'correct' or, if you wish, 'patriotic' interpretation of specific regimes, wars or revolutions.[17] The aim of history is to understand and explain past events. Memory, on the other hand, is 'the knowledge of what is good, what is bad, and what is neither good nor bad'.[18] Memory helps individuals to find meaning in their lives and to create bonds of solidarity with other people. Collective and individual memories are two sides of the same coin, because individual memories are shaped through interactions with other people and reflect dominant discourses of society.[19]

Politics is largely about shaping collective memories, and these memories either glorify or demonize alternative futures, both those immediate and those in the far distance. Politicians do not distinguish between memory and history. They influence collective memory to put forward a rigid version of what they call history. Their 'creative' interpretation of the past helps them to create a plausible narrative, identify role models and rationalize impending measures. As the Chinese President Xi Jinping put it: 'Through the mirror of history we gain a foresight into the future . . . We can see why we were successful in the past and why we will continue to succeed in the future.'[20]

Autocrats control the flow of information and ideas much more than democrats, but their manipulation of the past to project the future does not need to be crude. In fact, it is getting ever more sophisticated, according to Sergei Guriev and Daniel Treisman. In their 2022 book, Guriev and Treisman coined the term 'spin autocrats' to show that modern politicians such as Vladimir Putin, Recep Tayyip Erdoğan and Viktor Orbán prefer to rely on concealed censorship and manufactured narratives than on fear and violence to make people follow their visions of the present and the future.[21] Democrats also need to construct historical narratives. Memories tell potential voters who they are and who they want to be. They tell voters who are friends, and who are enemies. They justify proposed sacrifices of blood and riches. In this sense, the historical dimension of time intrudes on our private lives and time too.

We can query whether in high-speed society memories are fading away and the time horizon of history is becoming shorter. However, the recent resurgence of 'history wars' across the globe suggests that memories and history will continue to be at the centre of political battles.[22] History wars may well spring up from below, but those at the top must steer them. This is because political careers are dependent on the dimension of historical time. It is hard to enjoy legitimacy without being in charge of the passage of time. To paraphrase George Orwell: whoever controls the past, controls the future. Political utopias hark back to an imagined Arcadian past, which the recent past may have betrayed, and which the future, under our guidance, will revive.[23] Thus, in the politics of memory, the past need not be glorious in order to help design a magnificent future. Historical failures and defeats may also justify a great leap forward towards a new, ideal future reflecting our 'unique' resilience and 'eternal' values.

Politicians not only canonize some historical figures as heroes and present others as villains. They also give symbolic meaning to historical events such as the 1389 Battle of Kosovo, the 1690 Battle of the Boyne, the 1815 defeat of Napoleon at Waterloo, the 1920 Trianon Treaty, the 1933 Reichstag Fire or the 1968 assassination of Martin Luther King. They propose competing periodizations of history and draw alternative visions for the future.

In contemporary Poland, political cleavages do not reflect class or party lines, but are linked to competing interpretations of history. Was Poland a prime victim of the Holocaust or one of its culprits? Is Lech Wałęsa a hero of Poland's struggle for freedom or an agent of the Communist secret service? Does the 1989 roundtable agreement between the Communists and Solidarność represent a symbol of liberation or betrayal? The replies to these questions are a good predictor of an individual's electoral preferences in Poland. In Italy those who say that the anti-Fascist resistance was a bloody civil war are unlikely to vote for left-wing parties. In the United States of America, those who vote for the Democrats are unlikely to argue that the South fought for sovereignty rather than slavery, for example.

If something from the past is being recycled in the present, then we are back to the future. The explosion of populism with a nativist twist has made this painfully obvious. Contemporary nativists construct the future by taking us back to the idealized era of sovereign nation-states with a simple

cultural identity. We are urged to rally around the national flag and scorn all those who look and think differently. Memorial days of remembrance once again gather huge, agitated crowds misinterpreting and misusing our common past for the purpose of shaping the future. Plain historical distortions – if not outright lies – are being propagated, and so we start to tremble each time collective memories are mentioned.

We should not allow historical lies to spread unabated within our respective societies.[24] However, we should also keep in mind that memories are part of our identities, and they are always artificially constructed to some degree. As Milan Kundera nicely reasoned, without memories our sense of time collapses 'until everything is forgotten by everyone'.[25] This is not what we want. Auschwitz should not be erased from our memory, nor even diminished in its significance. The same can be said about numerous other horrendous episodes in human history, no matter where you come from.

Standing up for our values will always involve a battle over memory, with its corresponding rituals, songs, slogans, statues and flags. We hope that this battle will give all of us a fair chance to present our interpretation of history. Yet despotic regimes try to make sure that citizens are unable to hear the 'noise of time', to use the title of Julian Barnes' novel about a famous Soviet-era composer, Dmitri Shostakovich. The Soviet Union is no longer around, which may suggest that engineering memories full of lies does not secure the future. Sadly, despotic regimes are still with us, and they are ever more adroit in using digital media for making us remember or forget certain aspects of our history.[26]

Don't look up!

History wars may help explain our failure to properly address the future, but so do certain aspects of modern democracy. It is enough to watch the 2021 satirical movie entitled *Don't Look Up* to understand why politics ignores the future.

The movie, directed by Adam McKay, is not a cinematic masterpiece, but the story it tells made it a topic of public debate across the globe. Why? Because the movie shows how politics sleepwalks into a disaster that could be avoided. The plot is simple but engaging. Two astronomers are attempting to warn the media and authorities about a huge, approaching comet that will destroy human civilization in six months. However, their message is either ignored, trivialized or hijacked for political and business purposes. The media tries to keep the terrifying story entertaining, the President tries to use the crisis to boost her popularity, and business barons try to earn money from the deadly comet. Political short-termism, social media gossip and the selfish fantasies of big tech are all on display, preventing any meaningful action to avert Armageddon. Although the scientists are '100 per cent for sure [we're all] gonna fucking die!' the prospect does not light a fire under decision-makers due to political expediency, financial greed and commonplace foolishness. There is no Hollywood happy ending on this occasion, and the planet is destroyed.

Conservative critics described the movie as 'a derivative and meandering "satire" of capitalism, Donald Trump, and climate deniers'.[27] Those on the left barked back that 'much of our political elite are just as greedy and foolish, our media just as vapid, and our response to impending disaster exactly as mind-bogglingly irrational as in the movie'.[28] More crucially, however, scientists found the story in the movie plausible, and reflective of their own experience. An American climate scientist, Peter Kalmus, found the 'terrifying non-response to climate breakdown' as pictured in the movie 'the most accurate' he had seen.[29] He added:

> After 15 years of working to raise climate urgency, I've concluded that the public in general, and world leaders in particular, underestimate how rapid, serious and permanent climate and ecological breakdown will be if humanity fails to mobilize.[30]

This is very much in line with what most scientists think about our failure to arrest climate change, and other possible calamities.[31] Why is the scientific evidence notoriously ignored, twisted, denied or downplayed? Should we blame ourselves, or deviant political institutions?

Politicians like to point fingers at us, the citizens. In a democracy we must reflect voters' preferences, they argue, and voters tend to be short-sighted and selfish. This may sound like a cheap excuse, but it is hard to deny that voters can be myopic, looking at events and policies that are close to their present-day concerns. The evidence for this thesis is patchy, however, and there are numerous examples of voters rewarding politicians with horizons exceeding a single electoral term.[32]

When we come across myopic voters, we must query their motives. Why do voters tend to be myopic? There are two common answers, and they do not point to voters' egoism or irrational behaviour. The first answer highlights the fluid and difficult-to-predict future. The longer the time horizon of adopted measures, the less certain the return on the investments made. It is quite rational to support policies that have a higher rather than lower probability of achieving their objectives. Betting money on an uncertain future is always risky, isn't it? The problem is that the notion of what is certain or uncertain in the future is relative and often subject to manipulation. Corporations making billions on environmentally hazardous policies conduct orchestrated PR campaigns to sow confusion in voters' minds regarding climate change. Scientific evidence regarding the danger of antibiotic resistance is often questioned by the agricultural lobby. Employers' associations tend to describe successive pension reforms as unaffordable, excessive, undermining competitiveness and stimulating unemployment. Governments are not innocent bystanders in this game. They finance some scientific studies and neglect or even silence others to justify their policies. They also contribute to the communicative muddle. For instance, a group of analysts and former diplomats accused Australian Prime Minister Scott Morrison of running a 'denialist government' using 'greenwash' to meet its emissions commitments.[33] This leads to the second reason behind voters' alleged myopia: they do not believe that governments will deliver on long-term commitments.

In most established democracies political distrust is now the norm, rather than the exception. Over 60 per cent of all Europeans claim not to trust their national parliament and national government.[34] In the US, 83 per cent of Americans claim that they 'never' or 'only some of the time' trust their government to do what is right.[35] No wonder that voters are reluctant to let governments spend huge sums of money on their behalf. Even if a given social or environmental project seems credible, there is no expectation that it can be delivered over the long run. Voters can discipline politicians within a single electoral term, but there is no guarantee that a new government will stick to commitments undertaken by the old one. Voters may also have good reasons to think that politicians are not competent enough to steer ambitious long-term projects, even if they are honest. However, in many countries the honesty of politicians is not taken for granted, which explains why public perceptions of corruption are closely correlated with the levels of distrust.

Our discussion about historical nostalgia suggests yet another reason for citizens' reluctance to embrace long-term policies. These policies imply not only financial costs, but also numerous psychological and behavioural adjustments, new modes of consumption, alternative energy sources or the reorganization of labour markets. In essence, addressing the challenges of the future signifies change, and voters may be keener to suppress rather than embrace change.

Change usually implies the end of stability and familiar order. Change generates new winners and losers. Change, if serious, amounts to a jump into the unknown. Many of us would rather keep things as they are, despite all manifestations of inefficiency and injustice. Successive notions of the 'end of history' have proved so tempting because so many people worship the status quo. Many of us have embraced calls to 'bring our state back' because the state is a symbol of stability and familiar order. Nationalism is in vogue again because it limits remedies and rewards to a small group of co-nationals with whom we share a culture and history. Those decrying the loss of sovereignty and national unity usually scorn ecologists, virologists, microbiologists – even cyclists and vegans – because all these categories demand embracing change rather than the status quo. The more people are pressed to embrace epochal change – be it in the field of the environment, health, technology or social provisions – the more they dig themselves into parochial holes. This is one of the reasons why conservative politicians are thriving at present, not only on the right, but also on the left of the political spectrum.

High-speed capitalism and culture only reinforce this resistance to change, because in a high-speed society changes are more prominent than ever. As a result, the future is being ignored or even suppressed. The danger of things going badly wrong in the future is being underplayed. Our capacity to handle eventual catastrophes is being declared with pathetic, and unmerited, confidence. Advocates of even modest changes are framed as ideologically brainwashed fanatics. The politics of nostalgia reigns. Actions to avert the collapse of the pension system, climate change or traffic congestion are being mimicked, with no real intention to deliver any meaningful adjustments.

Of course, these are sweeping generalizations, because citizens do not have uniform visions of the future and related interests. Age, education, wealth, gender and race are important factors, drawing complex maps of convergence and divergence. In John Osborne's 1956 play *Look Back in Anger*, the main protagonist, Alison, tells her father how he differs from her husband, Jimmy. 'You're hurt because everything's changed, and Jimmy's hurt because everything's stayed the same.'[36] Another memorable line manifesting diverging perceptions of the future was the *gilets jaunes'* slogan during their 2018 revolt in France: 'The elites are talking about the end of the world and we are talking about the end of the month.' And I will never forget a conversation with a friend in Jakarta when I complained about the pollution caused by traffic in that vibrant city. 'Don't you want to breathe fresh air?' I asked. He replied disarmingly, 'Of course I want to, but I need to get to work somehow or else I cannot feed my children. For you in Oxford using a car is a matter of choice, while for me it is a matter of survival.' Clearly, we are not all in the same boat sailing through these stormy waters, which means that our hopes and fears regarding the future are not in sync.

Can democracy safeguard the future?

Democracy is supposed to sort out our different perceptions, interests and needs so as to allow a concerted effort to tackle the future. Sadly, this supposition sounds increasingly over-optimistic, if not naive. To start with, democracy is a system attached to nation-states, which means that democracy in the UK or US can hardly address problems facing my friend in Jakarta. In the absence of a cosmopolitan democracy, we are unable to bridge diverging perceptions of the future across the globe. This is particularly troubling because most of the epochal challenges are transnational, while the notion of transnational democracy remains a myth on a global level, and perhaps even on a European one. In a world that is 'shrinking' because of accelerated speed and 'imploding' because of intensified interdependence, the absence of any supranational democracy is puzzling indeed.[37]

When it comes to the future, democracy also performs poorly in our respective states. In a book from which I have borrowed the title of this section, Graham Smith is quite explicit: 'Democracies have a blind spot when it comes to the long term. From issues such as pensions, health and social care, and infrastructure through to climate change, biodiversity, pandemics, and emerging technologies, we find repeated failures to develop robust policies that safeguard the interests of future generations.'[38]

The most common explanation for these failures is that future generations do not vote in today's elections. Democracy by its nature reflects the interests, needs and perceptions of those who have the right to cast a vote at the ballot box today. The problem is that the electoral calendar hardly ever corresponds with the calendar required for addressing long-term challenges. And when decisions taken by present-day governments seriously affect future generations they effectively 'colonize' and disempower them.[39] If the current generation damages the climate beyond repair, the future generation is effectively doomed – or cooked, to put it literally. The same path dependency will be at work if the current generation fails to bring AI under control, makes huge financial debts or erodes the sustainability of the pension system. Not only policies of benign neglect but also positive ones pose severe constraints on future generations. Consider, for instance, decisions to opt for nuclear power stations or to join military alliances such as the CSTO (Collective Security Treaty Organization, led by Russia). Are states free to

quit the CSTO? Do we know how to handle increased nuclear waste?[40]

Electoral calendars also create perverse incentives for politicians to focus on the present. I use the term 'calendars' in the plural because democracy envisages regular elections to various branches and units of government, which means that politicians are campaigning around the clock. National legislative elections are followed by local elections, those in turn by presidential elections, and we also have mid-term or by-elections in some states, and European elections on the old continent. When I was studying British politics in the 1970s I came across a catchy phrase attributed to Prime Minister Harold Wilson: 'A week is a long time in politics.' In the media-saturated world of today, even 24 hours is a lifetime in politics.

We often blame the media and opinion polls for politicians' short-sightedness, but their rushing about and flashy behaviour is a function of democracy and its narrow time perspective. Maximizing short-term gains at the expense of long-term progress is a democratic predicament, I am afraid. Even if relatively small investments in huge future gains are considered, democracy stumbles. This is not always comprehended by scientists urging politicians to invest in sensible long-term projects. 'The investment of $40 billion over ten years for the world to avoid a $100 trillion cost by 2050 should make any finance minister stand up and take note,' argue three experts in their book on the deadly spread of superbugs.[41] I fear that most ministers of finance are likely to choke when asked to put billions of dollars on the table as advised by these experts. Even if they are scared of superbugs, they must also listen to their ministerial colleagues demanding money for soldiers, teachers, police officers and even failed bankers.

My critique of democracy's short-term horizon does not mean that democracy cannot get anything right. As David Runciman has persuasively argued, democracies are bad at avoiding emergencies, but good at recovering from them, at least in the immediate term, I may add.[42] Communist states' obsession with long-term planning generated less overall prosperity than democratic states' short-termism. In the absence of democratic accountability embodied by periodic elections there is no guarantee that long-term policies will do any good. However, we should not jump to definite conclusions. Contemporary China's reliance on long-term vision and planning is often quoted as the reason for its impressive growth. And there is evidence suggesting that technocracy performs better than democracy even in some Western states. Italy was praised by the international press and markets when led by the technocratic governments of Mario Monti and Mario Draghi, even though (or perhaps because) they did not enjoy popular electoral mandates.[43]

The Italian case reveals experts' favourite recipes for conducting long-term projects in a myopic democracy.[44] Decision-making powers ought to be delegated to institutions, which by design are not directly accountable to voters or their elected representatives. These are so-called non-majoritarian institutions such as central banks, constitutional courts and numerous regulatory agencies, national or international. Central banks can reduce reckless governmental spending affecting future generations. Constitutional courts can guard the laws protecting minorities, the environment and social welfare. Regulatory agencies can make sure that the production of food, medicines or vehicles is sustainable and safe. The European Commission can spend money for long-term projects such as development aid that would be blocked by national parliaments in member states.[45]

However, before we get too enthusiastic about delegating powers to experts, we ought to ask some basic questions. Is it fair to disempower the current generation of voters on behalf of the future generation of voters?[46] And why should scientists and technocrats decide what is 'right' for the future, and not democratically elected politicians? The former may have superior expertise, but they are not free from ideological prejudices and corporate lobbying. In fact, there is ample evidence suggesting that the future-oriented megaprojects proposed by experts often fail to measure up to the lofty and lavish claims made in their defence.[47] Although these projects are accompanied by bombastic PR campaigns, they are seldom transparent and rarely reach their conclusion because of accumulated debts, poor planning or even corruption.[48] Consider Ciudad Real International Airport in Spain, the NHS Civilian IT project in the UK, Yucca Mountain Nuclear Waste Repository in the US or Poland's Turów power plant expansion.[49] We should not dismiss out of hand the construction of new power stations, airports, digital communication systems and even weapons. But the decisions to invest huge sums of money in these projects cannot be conducted behind closed doors by a narrow group of civil servants, lobbyists and experts.

The excessive delegation of powers to non-majoritarian institutions transforms democracy into oligarchy. In an oligarchy, citizens may well be able to change a government, but they are not able to change policies, because policies endorsed by voters will be vetoed by judges, bankers, the IMF or the EU. I do not endorse tabloid headlines describing eurocrats, bankers and judges as 'enemies of the people', but as a citizen I want to have a real voice, not just a meaningless vote. I do not endorse post-truth and science-bashing, but I believe that in a democracy people and their elected representatives should have the right to shape the notion of collective interests, and not unelected experts. Experts can reveal to citizens the pros and cons of nuclear energy, but decisions to opt in favour or against this kind of energy should be in the hands of citizens. Experts can disclose the implications of rising pensions or lowering the retirement age. Nevertheless, it is doubtful whether experts or even judges (let alone bankers) should be in a position to decide the retirement age or the scale of benefits.

For me, a solution for embracing the future is not less but more democracy. I trust my fellow citizens no less than I trust those who hold important offices. If you complain that my fellow citizens are reluctant to embrace long-term projects, you need to ask for their motivations. Maybe they do not feel part of these projects. Maybe they think that these projects benefit neither them nor their children. And if we think that democracy is no longer functional, let's reform it rather than dilute it. I will say more about this in the concluding chapter.

Reclaiming the future

Each generation has its favourite song about the future and flow of time. I entered university in 1973, the year Pink Floyd released their iconic album *The Dark Side of the Moon*, featuring the song 'Time'. The lyrics written by the band's bassist, Roger Walters, urged us to take control of our destiny or else risk missing 'the starting gun'.[50] This song, and numerous others, makes me wonder whether citizens do indeed ignore the future and the need to carefully time their actions to save the future. On the contrary, we seem to be obsessed with the future. We try to obtain a permanent job to secure the future, save money and augment our pension funds. We send children to school to seal their prospects, often paying a lot of money to give them the best chances, years in the future. We even eat and exercise with the future in mind, because we want to live longer. To argue that our personal concern about the future does not extend to public life sounds to me like a sweeping exaggeration. Think about impressive waves of citizens' mobilization in defence of peace, the natural environment, women's rights or racial justice. Young people, in particular, seem to follow Pink Floyd's counsel.[51] However, we want to invest our time and money in projects that we can trust and shape in meaningful ways. Therefore, our willingness to face the future collectively depends on the quality of democracy and is not necessarily a function of our alleged presentism.

Of course, citizens in autocratic states may have different perspectives and priorities. However, studies of civic resistance in quite diverse states that used to be autocratic, such as Greece, South Korea, Poland or Tunisia, show that democracy is seen as the best vehicle for protecting human rights, economic sustainability and human development.[52] The struggle for a better quality of democracy can only begin after the formal instalment of democratic institutions. Thousands of people regularly demonstrating on Poland's streets in defence of the rule of law, women's rights to abortion, or LGBT+ equal rights clearly believe that their future cannot be secured merely through elections and parliamentary representation.[53] Those who demonstrate may well have the vote, but they feel that they have no voice. Similar protests are being forged across the entire community of democracies, demanding more power to the ordinary people like you and me. Democracy that empowers oligarchs, rewards demagoguery, hype and spin, as well as generating accidental short-term fixes, is clearly not working for those taking to the streets.

The uncertainty surrounding the future does not explain our inaction either. Governments know that the global temperature increase needs to remain below 1.5 degrees Celsius, and yet they repeatedly miss this target. They are paranoid about prospects of mass migration and yet they are building futile walls while cutting development aid that could stem migration in the long run. They know that most pension systems are unsustainable, and yet they facilitate zero-hours contracts that make no provisions for pensions. They are familiar with threats posed by the frenetic rise of AI, and yet they do little about automated decision systems or cyber security. Of course, there are 'unknown unknowns', to cite Donald Rumsfeld, but politics notoriously ignores what Rumsfeld calls 'known knowns', no matter which individuals or parties are in charge of our states.[54] Clearly, this has something to do with our system of democratic governance.

Blaming capitalism for short-termism also sounds like a sweeping exaggeration.[55] Stock markets may well be obsessed with a present that is measured in seconds rather than years, but most firms make long-term investments, especially if operating in a stable regulatory environment. Regulations are a matter of democracy, its fairness and effectiveness. It's true that our measures of success often value short-term economic return and rapid consumption. However, the way we assess economic success and failure is not set in stone. Democracies are free to change their indicators and create incentives for long-term economic projects and sustainable development.

Proposals aimed at making democracy less myopic tend to focus on institutions. We could emulate Finland or Israel and create special bodies with a mandate to oversee the long-term implications of adopted policies and enhance sustainable thinking among policy-makers.[56] The Hungarian Ombudsman for Future Generations and New Zealand's Children's and Retirement Commissioners have also played important roles in making their governments focus on the future.[57] (A United Nations High Commissioner for the Future has also been suggested.) We could create bodies enhancing our strategic foresight capabilities such as the Forward Studies Unit (*Cellule de Prospective*) created by the European Commission after the fall of the Berlin Wall.[58] We could revamp the institutions in charge of regulation and infrastructure planning. We could even adopt a special law demanding public institutions to think about the long-term.[59] However, institutions in charge of the future can only perform their functions well in a healthy political environment. As Jonathan Boston rightly observed in his monumental study on governing the future:

In terms of institutions, good long-term public governance requires all the conditions needed for good governance in general: robust, effective, and accountable democratic institutions; a competent, efficient, non-partisan bureaucracy; an independent judiciary; reliable and comprehensive data; capable, diligent, and trustworthy political leaders; low levels of corruption; a vibrant, informed civil society; and a vigorous, free, independent, and responsible fourth estate.[60]

Boston's comments suggest that institutional engineering, however useful, will not produce wonders by itself. Reclaiming the future demands a fundamental reform of our respective polities and the way we move forward. As we have shown earlier in this chapter, pressure is mounting to focus on the past rather than the future, or to address the future with the help of the same failed institutional solutions. In reality, we will need to handle both the past and the future, but in a different way than by erecting and destroying historical monuments. As Helga Nowotny perceptively put it:

> The future will be dominated by digital technologies while we simultaneously face a sustainability crisis ... Digital technologies bring the future into the present, while the sustainability crisis confronts us with the past and challenges us to develop new capabilities for the future.[61]

I am not sure that nation-states can be revived and if so, whether they will manage to secure the future in a world exceeding their spatial and temporal horizons. This is not only because I fear nativist politicians calling for a *renaissance* of nation-states, but also because states are not up to the challenge, especially if they act on their own. Entertaining nostalgia for empire as a way of ordering the world seems even more dangerous.[62] The next chapter will shed more light on spatial governance, so let me conclude with a few short recommendations. First of all, we need to reclaim the future from the guardians of the status quo responsible for astronomic inequalities, environmental catastrophe and the misuse of digital technologies. We also need to identify a vision of the future that is not based on prejudice, exclusion, falsified history and the ruthless exploitation of our biosphere. We should then 'empower the spaces for participation and deliberation', to use Graham Smith's words.[63] A collective future must involve all of us and not only politicians and experts. The shape of the future should emerge from conversation and not from ready-made blueprints, however well intentioned. These are simple, but radical recommendations, suggesting that the future is in your hands, dear reader. Don't miss the starting gun, especially if you are young!

7

FROM STATES TO NETWORKS

In 2021 the European Council on Foreign Relations (ECFR) reported that most people surveyed believed that networks are more influential than hegemonic states such as the United States or China.[1] They pointed fingers particularly at the network of billionaires allegedly running the world with no atomic weapons or tanks at their disposal. They could just as well point fingers at you and me, because we are also part of a variety of networks. Some of us are on Twitter or Facebook, while others are part of professional, local or family networks connected in forms that are more traditional or hybrid. Does this make us influential? The answer depends on the context and issue. Bill Gates is one of the billionaires suspected of manipulating the networked world behind the scenes. Yet when in his 2015 TED talk he urged to prepare for a huge viral pandemic, his counsel was ignored by governments.[2] Clearly, Gates' influence proved to have some limits when compared with 'sovereign' states. States have also ignored similar warnings about the pandemic raised by virologists from renowned academic networks. How many lives could have been saved had governments listened to these networks? Numerous think-tanks and NGOs also warned that Russia's President Putin held an expansionist agenda vis-à-vis Ukraine as manifested by the illegal annexation of Crimea and parts of the Donbas in 2014. They called on European states, in particular, to reduce their dependence on Russian oil and gas, but states such as Italy increased rather than decreased their imports from Russia after 2014. We now know the price of this dependence.

These two sad cases made many of us conclude that those at the helm of our states are indifferent and incompetent. However, I wonder whether the problem is not more funda-mental. Perhaps power is located in the wrong place. Perhaps we have entrusted states and their governments with tasks they are not able to perform well. For the past three centuries or so, states have been in charge of regulating time and space. States decided how freely we can move across space, how long we can be asked to work, when we can wed or retire. Before the rise of nation-states, time and space were regulated by a variety of civic and religious authorities with a different spatial reach: the Church, the Empire, the city, the principality or the guild to mention but a few. States came to political prominence by setting and reinforcing borders and by ruling within these borders in a 'sovereign' manner. The notion of public time and its intrusion into our private, if not intimate, personal time has also been decreed by states. By asserting formal powers over time and space, states made themselves responsible for safeguarding our future. If we tend to lose faith in the future, this must be related to the capacity of states to shape this future. Perhaps the ECFR survey cited earlier suggests that many of us now believe that modern digital networks can better safeguard our future than traditional bureaucratic territorial states.

You may say that I am excessively provocative, if not demagogical. We all benefit from the security provided by states, and states, not networks, have institutions envisaging democracy and the rule of law. Can the future look bright without these 'goods' provided by states? But if states are indeed so good at providing security, why is there so much insecurity within and across states' borders? If states are bastions of democracy, why do so many of us feel that our vote does not count? If states are effective guardians of law, why can so much injustice be observed in our daily lives? Are we not idealizing nation-states, and giving them undue powers for running our lives? If states are meant to be strong and important, why do they appear so weak and inept?

But please do not misunderstand me. I do not intend to rehearse the old debate about the withering away of states. States are here to stay for many years to come, but their nature is constantly fluctuating, with implications for their legitimacy and effectiveness. We therefore need to understand what states can do well at present, and what can be managed better by other actors such as cities, regions or international agencies. Nor do I intend to rehearse the old debate about the relative virtues of the private and public sectors, the former exemplified by firms and the latter by states. The public function of states will not become redundant any time soon; even neoliberals understand that we need the public sector to take care of matters that do not generate instant profits. And who, if not states, will bail out irresponsible banks or firms when they cause a crisis? My objective is different, and one may say modest. I would like to establish what kind of public authority could help us regain control over the future in a world increasingly unbounded and interdependent. If we want to get to grips with time and space, we need to query the existing system of governance, which formally gives states an effective monopoly on violence, law-making and the day-to-day management of public affairs.[3] Are states in the best position to provide public goods in a world of hyper-connectivity and incessant digital communication? Can other actors make a valuable contribution to public governance, and if so, which ones exactly? Can authority be split or shared, and if so, how? Can informal networks be made accountable and subject to law?

I intend to compare the world of states with the world of networks because they offer contrasting approaches to governing time and space. The spatial domain of states is chiefly physical, while contemporary networks operate largely in the digital space. The world of states envisages a hierarchical spatial architecture, while the world of networks envisages a horizontal one. States organize space through physical borders and formal institutions, while networks put emphasis on informal communication and trans-border connectivity. Informal networks can act more quickly than bureaucratic states, which does not necessarily imply short-termism. As pointed out in the previous chapter, the electoral cycle in democratic states makes them biased in favour of the present, at the expense of the future. This explains why networks of cities and NGOs are often more genuinely committed to long-term future objectives such as climate change.

Of course, the world of states and the world of networks represent intellectual paradigms that simplify a messy reality on the ground. However, we need paradigms to map ongoing changes. The statist paradigm dominated our thinking about politics for many decades, but in recent years, states have faced hefty 'competition' from mysterious networks, and suddenly our perception of politics has begun to evolve. How can we explain this change?

The world of networks

Networks are as old as humanity, so why has the twenty-first century been hailed as the Age of Networks? This is because, thanks to the internet, the scale and speed of networked operations have assumed shocking dimensions. The internet has created a new galaxy of not just technological connections, but also social, cultural, economic and political ones.[4] Contemporary discussions about networks are therefore tied to discussions about the pros and cons of the internet, and by extension about the 'new kid on the block', namely artificial intelligence (AI).

172

Professor Niall Ferguson, who has studied the history of networks, has made us realize that networks are much older than digital technology or neoliberal ideology.[5] He points to the fact that humans have been organized into hierarchical structures for most of recorded history, with chiefs, lords, kings or emperors at the top of these hierarchies. People on the lower rungs of these structures were mainly connected locally through their respective family, village or church. Ferguson has shown that these networks were not only confined to tiny spaces, but they were also oppressive towards members lower down on the hierarchical ladder. The internet has not only opened up the traditional networked spaces, but it has also crushed existing hierarchies, introducing multiple vertical connections, and subsequently creating new power structures.

Given the wealth and influence currently enjoyed by internet companies such as Amazon, Alphabet (Google), Meta (Facebook) or the Chinese Tencent, we may be tempted to conclude that one type of hierarchy has been replaced by another.[6] However, it is difficult to deny that the internet has 'liberated numerous individuals from the grip of traditional families, villages and churches, for better or worse. Of course, today as in the Middle Ages there are also non-hierarchical, horizontal networks such as those between artists or universities.[7] The internet has clearly facilitated their links and increased their usefulness, if not their influence.

Manuel Castells has explained well why networks powered by the internet are 'superior' to their historical predecessors.

The internet has allowed networks to overcome their major shortcomings: the difficulty in coordinating their functions, in focusing resources on specific public goals, and moving beyond a limited, spatially constrained size. The internet has helped networks to coordinate tasks and manage complexity in a way that is novel if not superior to those employed by hierarchical, heavily institutional states. Networks are now able to utilize their traditional assets such as speed, flexibility, inclusiveness and adaptability without sacrificing a certain degree of command, control and coordination. The result is, to use Castells' own words, an 'unprecedented combination of flexibility and task performance, of coordinated decision-making and decentralized execution, of individualized expression and global, horizontal communication, which provide a superior form of human action'.[8]

The conceptualization of networks proves tricky, however. If we define networks as a set of interconnected nodes, then everything can represent a network, from a group of friends on Facebook to a clandestine cell of jihadists, an informal consortium of bankers or an Alcoholics Anonymous comradery.[9] States can also form various networks based on common values or expediency.[10] If networks are everywhere and anything can form a network, then we are living in a truly mysterious, or even confused world. Some academics have therefore distinguished between networks as structures and networks as actors.[11] The former represent constructions that influence the behaviour of their members, and through them produce given effects. The latter represent specific organizational forms that differ from hierarchies or markets.

Scholars have also identified various types of networks: social, economic and political, most notably. Computer science identifies a variety of Area Networks: Personal, Local, Metropolitan, Wide, Storage, Wireless, Peer-to-Peer and Virtual, to mention a few examples. Social scientists talk about simple and multi-layered networks, coherent and random, cells, cliques and coteries, tributaries, allies, accomplices and helpers.[12] They also differentiate between networks with weak and strong ties, or with a different degree of centrality. Some cultural sociologists tend to focus on different substantive attributes (for example, networks of speed dating tend to give premium to physical rather than intellectual attributes). Others focus on different preferential attachments (for example, rich people tend to stick with other rich individuals).[13]

We may feel frustrated reviewing the ever-growing literature on networks, but we should keep in mind that states are neither simple nor straightforward either. Germany and Cyprus may both belong to one integrated region, yet they are anything but similar in terms of size, wealth, cultural profile or security preoccupations. The gap between states such as China and Panama is even greater. Students of states, like those of networks, construct multifaceted typologies. They talk about authoritarian and democratic states, federal and confederal, republican and monarchical, nuclear and neutral, strong (or even hegemonic) and failed states. One can multiply similar examples. The monopoly on violence within a given territory is a matter of degree in individual states, and so is the ability to control external state borders. States' claim to legal, let alone factual, sovereignty is no more than 'organized hypocrisy'.[14]

Our knowledge of states is immensely more advanced than the knowledge of networks, but this does not make the latter less significant. Networks have been studied for a much shorter period than states, which means that our conceptual tools to analyse networks are still embryonic in comparison.[15] We also lack statistical data on networks because most of the data collected is still on states only. It is enough to look at the data published by diverse institutions such as the UK Office for National Statistics, Eurostat or the United Nations Statistics Division to see how much more we know about states as compared to networks. This does not mean that we are totally in the dark when talking about networks. Political analysts have studied networks to understand matters as diverse as interest groups, protest politics, banking regulations and terrorism. Network analysis has proved particularly useful in enhancing our knowledge of urban politics, international organizations, European integration and NGO activism. There is a growing body of empirical evidence suggesting that cities and NGOs in particular are skilful networkers, able to complement, frustrate or even replace states in meeting their policy objectives. Is this good or bad news?

The answer depends on the way networks exercise their influence. Power can always cause evil, but it is hard to do any good without power either. It is also important to establish who controls networks, and how. The legitimacy of networks, like that of any other sites of power, can also be questioned. As we discover that rule-making power is increasingly in the 'hands' of networks, the pressure to scrutinize networks grows with each day. The IT companies running social networking platforms in particular have come under public examination, partly because of their unprecedented spatial reach and partly because of their enormous wealth.

Xanadu: a perfect place?

For fans of the Electric Light Orchestra (ELO), *Xanadu* is the title of the successful 1980 movie featuring Olivia Newton-John, with a soundtrack composed and performed by the ELO. For students of social media, however, Xanadu is a term coined by Ted Nelson in 1965 to describe the universal hypermedia system he envisaged. Nelson argued that it would become possible to digitally store anything that anyone would write, record, photograph or film, and to produce a system that could connect any piece of information to any other piece of information. This vision he called Xanadu.[16]

Both versions of Xanadu were about making your dreams come true by going to places where nobody earlier dared to venture. This was also the ambition of Steve Jobs, the legendary co-founder of Apple. In his efforts 'to put a computer in the hands of everyday people' he adopted a *Xanadu*-like motto: Dream Bigger.[17]

The dream envisaged by Nelson, Jobs and creators of the worldwide net such as Tim Berners-Lee or Robert Cailliau is now part of our daily life, but we are not entirely sure whether this Xanadu is indeed a perfect place. Some would even argue that this dream is our worst nightmare. We may concede that the internet has made our lives easier and assisted scientific progress, but internet-generated networks are increasingly coming under fire. If we examine the critique carefully, however, networks are guilty only by association.

To begin with, a great deal of this anxiety is caused by the technology that powers networks. The information technology (IT) and artificial intelligence (AI) that raise legitimate concerns are not only utilized by networks, although one can claim that networks are more skilful in applying them.[18] Is there evidence suggesting that networks are using modern technology more harmfully than states, for instance? I don't think so. Consider how China is utilizing the internet for policing its citizens. The use and misuse of the PRISM or PEGASUS surveillance systems suggests that democratic states are also tempted to spy on their citizens.[19] The WikiLeaks case is often mentioned as an example manifesting the hazardous misuse of the internet by networks, but I wonder who is more dangerous in this case: the state abusing its power with the help of the internet, or the network revealing this

abuse on the internet? IT and AI, like all technologies, can be used by the good and bad guys, by legitimate organizations and by criminal ones, by scientists and by conspiracy theorists. Networks have benefited from the latest technology that offers incredibly fast connectivity with no geographic boundaries, but this does not make them responsible for all the supposed downsides of the latest inventions. The railway apparently dismantled village communities, the printed press perverted democracy and television eroded family life. Does this sound familiar?

The use and misuse of sophisticated algorithms has also raised legitimate concerns. With the help of algorithms, banks and insurance companies are scrutinizing our connections on

Facebook and Twitter to see who is 'worth' a loan or insurance cover, for instance. Breaches of privacy are not the only problem related to this practice. One wonders who makes the decisions here – humans, or computers applying algorithms? Do we trust AI? Are we sure that the data used by computers are relevant and complete? What if computer programs reflect our class or racial biases? And most worryingly, will AI escape human control? Will robots turn on us?

These are not simply questions posed by people watching too many movies featuring aggressive avatars such as *The Terminator* or *The Matrix*. Famous scientists such as Stephen Hawking have said that 'the development of full artificial intelligence could spell the end of the human race'. [20] One of the planet's most successful entrepreneurs, Elon Musk, has declared that AI is humanity's 'biggest existential threat'.[21] As algorithms are ever more widely applied in designing education, marketing and public services, we start to wonder who is really in charge. Imagine if robots controlled by AI acquired personalities, formed distinct interests from humans and started to advance their own well-being. Would they not pose dangers to our existence?[22]

Fears of this sort are not new. Two writers from Prague, Franz Kafka and Karel Čapek, expressed them vividly as long as a century ago. Kafka, in his 1925 book *The Trial*, tells the story of Josef K., a respectable bank officer arrested and prosecuted by a remote, inaccessible authority, with the nature of his crime revealed neither to him nor to the reader. The book is usually described as a prophecy of the mad excesses of modern bureaucracy bordering on totalitarianism, but today it reads like a description of the world governed by advanced algorithms and artificial intelligence. The 2001 Vintage Classics edition of the book has a telling cover that features a kind of network.[23] Karel Čapek's 1920 drama entitled *Rossum's Universal Robots* was even more suggestive in articulating contemporary fears prompted by AI advances. The drama is about the manufacture of artificial people from synthetic organic material to free humans from work and drudgery, but due to overproduction these 'roboti' lead humankind to destruction.[24] (In fact, the term 'robot' was first coined by Čapek.)

In the 1920s the internet was not yet known, and the term 'artificial intelligence' was not in use. Perhaps these two writers grasped the human anxieties related to all kinds of technological progress that we unleash and then fail to keep in check. However, control is not just a matter of technical capabilities. As Helga Nowotny argued: 'There is an overestimation of the technology and an underestimation of the social contexts in which AI is operating, whose interests it serves, and in which political and economic circumstances.'[25] Nowotny therefore pleads for human values and perspectives to be the starting point for the design of digital systems that 'claim to serve humanity'.[26] In other words, the focus ought to be on us rather than AI. We humans practised despotism long before the era of algorithms. So far, the greatest atrocities have been committed by us humans, not robots. We first need to get our norms right and then create a governance system able to spread these values. Technology can help or hinder our ambitions, it can be used or abused, depending on our own choices and behaviour. There is no point blaming technology for our own human failings.

Much of the fire is aimed at tech giants operating social media platforms where the bulk of networks are located. IT companies promised an open system, but they installed a closed system controlled by a handful of monopolies (Facebook, Amazon and Google) and duopolies (Microsoft and Apple).[27] Incredible fortunes have been made by offering free-of-charge access and world-wide connectivity in return for personal information that could be utilized by advertisers. Deception, manipulation and the unscrupulous quest for profit is said to be a trademark of these companies, with little regard for the lofty principles featured on their official websites. This criticism seems to me to be justified, but it also applies to most huge companies operating in global markets. It is enough to review the scandals surrounding firms such as Enron, Volkswagen, General Electric, Lockheed or the Lehman Brothers to realize that a certain kind of predatory behaviour is part of modern capitalism and can hardly be attributed only to tech giants. In a less permissive regulatory environment this kind of behaviour would be costly rather than rewarding. Why do states that see themselves as key regulators fail to break up these platforms and curb targeted advertising, for instance? Are they unwilling or unable to regulate internet platforms? Strong federal data privacy legislation, enforcing antitrust laws and restoring net neutrality have all been topics of debate in the United States for some time already, with no resolution in sight. Social media giants, Facebook in particular, have also been accused of interfering in elections, but again, this deplorable behaviour can be attributed to many other kinds of companies (and states). Moreover, can we blame the social networks operating on Facebook for the misbehaviour of Facebook as a company? True, they could move their network to another platform, but only rich people such as Donald Trump can afford to create their own digital platform to make sure that it reflects 'truth'.[28]

The way social networks communicate in the digital space has come under fire, and quite understandably. It is hard to deny that we can find many ethically deplorable opinions on Twitter, Instagram or Facebook, but I wonder whether we can blame the internet platforms or the social networks themselves for these opinions.[29] This would be like blaming a post office in the 'good old days' for delivering letters full of racially motivated hatred. When I was young, living on the 'wrong' side of the Iron Curtain, the post office indeed controlled and censored letters. Fortunately, democracies came to believe that education is a better way to combat extremism than censorship. Besides, do we trust the internet companies to do the job of censoring the content of our exchanges? Consider how YouTube and Facebook censored artworks by the American painter and videographer, Grace Graupe-Pillard, for allegedly exhibiting her aged body.[30]

Social networking sites can offer extremists anonymity and a mass audience, which is a legitimate source of concern, but we should ask a series of fundamental questions. Why is there a market for extremism? Why do so many people not trust science? Why are we so terribly polarized on and off social media? Social media features not only extremists but also those combating extremism. The distinction between these two groups is not always clear, which only complicates any micro-management of online discourses. In the past, feminists and trade unionists were often portrayed as extremists. 'Terrorists' turned into 'freedom fighters'. And there are also technical barriers to steering online exchanges. Consider the limited effectiveness of the Russian and Chinese efforts to control discussions on the internet.

Networks that matter

We tend to focus on criminal or terrorist networks in the same way that we focus on flawed or failed states. Well-functioning states such as Switzerland or Norway are seldom sexy enough to make the headlines, but they offer unusual prosperity and security to their citizens. Networks making a valuable contribution to public governance are certainly more boring than secret masons or jihadist cells, but they are making the world a better place by assisting or replacing states in their traditional roles. Who are they? On my own merit list, first place is occupied by NGOs campaigning for noble societal goals such as protecting human rights, alleviating poverty, arresting climate change or enhancing transparency. Most of these goals are transnational in nature, which explains why NGOs connect across borders with their audiences and partners. NGOs usually try to engage directly with the general public, but they are more than happy to join forces with governments supporting their cause. They are also happy to form partnerships with firms. For instance, Oxfam has teamed up with Nokia and Marks & Spencer, and Greenpeace with Unilever and Coca-Cola. Even the anti-corporate Occupy Wall Street has taken donations from business leaders.[31]

Links between firms and NGOs do not end here. This is because business associations should probably be included in the broad family of NGOs. Unlike specific firms, they campaign for collective rather than individual or private causes. The same can be said about international trade union federations such as the International Trade Union Confederation, UNI Global Union, Education International or the International Federation of Journalists. The long list of business associations includes some of the most potent political players such as the US Chamber of Commerce, the International Organization of Employers, the European Banking Federation and the World Economic Forum. Are they solely committed to 'good' public causes? I am not sure, but I refuse the unqualified assumption that all those associated with money-making have dirty hands. Individual networks ought to be judged on their own record of performance and there is no simple notion of good and evil in most cases.

The hybrid and sometimes fuzzy nature of NGOs has led to typologies with an impressive number of fancy acronyms:

QUANGOs (quasi-governmental organizations), GONGOs (government-organized NGOs), PONGOs (parliament-organized NGOs or, sometimes, personal NGOs), FINGOs (financially interested NGOs), GANGOs (gap-filling NGOs), BRINGOs (briefcase NGOs), DONGOs (donor-organized NGOs), DINGOs (donor international NGOs), BONGOs (business-organized NGOs), BINGOs (business-interest NGOs), BENGOs (bent, in the sense of crooked, NGOs), CHONGOs (city-hall NGOs), GRINGOs (government-run or – inspired NGOs), PANGOs (party-affiliated NGOs), RONGOs (retired-officials NGOs) and COMENGOs (come and go, or here today and gone tomorrow, NGOs).[32] These different NGOs have several features in common: they usually operate in an informal mode with no strong institutional hierarchy, and the internet is their main platform to inform and mobilize their audiences.

Cities also form viable networks engaged in public causes.[33] The majority of the world's population lives in cities nowadays, and the figure in the developed part of the world will soon be 80 per cent. No wonder that urban governments determine our lives to a large extent. Most public provisions are now administered by cities rather than states. Large cities, in particular, are multi-ethnic and multinational hotspots where global trades, lawyers and bankers mix with locals and migrants.[34] Connectivity is therefore part of their DNA.[35] Even our sense of security is now being shaped by cities, if only because petty criminals, political extremists and terrorists are operating in cities rather than villages.

Cities, unlike regions and states, are not particularly interested in representing a nation, claiming 'sovereign' rights across multiple fields or raising borders demarcating their own territory. They are instead, to use Benjamin Barber's words, 'interactive web flows in which interdependence is the key factor driving culture, trade, immigration, transportation, and other inter-city activities'.[36] This explains why cities tend to operate as networks relying on informal, horizontal connections aimed at addressing individual problems rather than gaining formal prerogatives.

Not all cities are smart, safe and prosperous, although some of them are larger and more resourceful than medium-sized states. While it is true that urban governments are closer to ordinary people than national governments, there is no evidence suggesting that local politicians are less prone to political patronage and corruption than national politicians. Nor is it true that mayors make good prime ministers. Consider Matteo Renzi of Italy or Boris Johnson of the UK. Yet it is hard to deny the role urban networks play in strengthening local democracy, generating innovation (especially in the environmental field), accommodating migrants, combating poverty and enhancing education. Today, cities play an important role in linking their local and national economies with global hubs. By doing this, they generate 'new geographies of centrality', to use Saskia Sassen's words.[37] In her view, the management and servicing of much of the global economic system takes place through cities because they possess distinctive resources able to accommodate ever-growing 'geographic dispersal and mobility'.[38]

Numerous cities are also cultural agents on a global scale, with their tourist attractions and lifestyle trendsetters. Governance practised by cities is usually more transparent, consensual, sustainable and efficient than the governance offered by states. Civic engagement is pronounced in urban governance and so is the use of digital technologies. Consider, for instance, the New Municipalism in Barcelona or Public-Common Partnerships in Manchester.[39] All these characteristics make cities well suited for the 'age of networks' in which the ability to innovate, connect, delegate and turn interdependence into an asset are keys for success. Urban networks such as the Global Parliament of Mayors, the C40 Cities Climate Leadership Group, and 100 Resilient Cities are already institutionalized, and are reminiscent of the golden age of cities in the Middle Ages, embodied by the Hanseatic League.[40]

The third type of network contributing to public governance is set up by states, but not fully controlled by them. Some are based on formal treaties such as the European Union, while others are informal arrangements involving states, state agencies (usually regulators or central bankers), NGOs (advocacy groups or business associations), universities, cities or regions. The 'One Belt One Road' project, initiated and largely financed by China, is said to represent one such network of diverse actors engaged in multiple infrastructure projects, constructing ports and railroads, laying fibre cables and even launching satellites.[41] It takes inspiration from the Silk Road network linking the East and West during the Han Dynasty of

China in 130 BCE.[42] Like its historic forerunner, the One Belt One Road project is chiefly about connectivity, bringing China's academics, artists, mayors and entrepreneurs to distant and diverse places such as Greece, Sri Lanka and Tanzania. Whether this project is a threat or an opportunity for the non-Chinese partners is a contentious topic, but it is clear that the project represents a different form of engagement than traditional state-to-state diplomacy.[43]

Informal, non-binding networks gathering state and non-state actors proliferate even in the field of security. This is because states find them more useful than traditional diplomacy to foster arms control, weapons proliferation, and counterterrorism. Non-governmental bodies such as the International Institute for Strategic Studies in London or the Stockholm International Peace Research Institute act as attractive hubs for states, think-tanks and arms manufacturers to enhance their respective agendas. The Georgian Orthodox Church acted as an important hub for state officials and civil campaigners in diffusing conflicts between Georgia and Russia following the 2008 military clash in South Ossetia.[44] The informal network launched by President Bush in 2003 under the name Proliferation Security Initiative has probably tackled the spread of weapons of mass destruction more effectively than formal state-to-state arrangements conducted under the United Nations' institutional umbrella.[45]

The European Union is also a kind of network, with Brussels acting like a concentrated point of intersection and interaction rather than a commanding centre. Although the EU is based on a formal treaty, with (member) states at the steering wheel, its structure and mode of engagement are not hierarchical in any sense. EU governance structure does not look like a pyramid, but rather a 'garbage can' with different cross-cutting policy networks operating without a straightforward division of power and chain of command.[46] EU institutions, member states and sub-states (cities and regions), transnational and supranational actors – all interact with each other in complex grids of varying horizontal and vertical density. EU governance is increasingly non-territorial, multilevel and multicentred. It is more about bargaining between different actors than about the automatic implementation of commands from the centre. This is because the large bulk of EU law is soft rather than hard, leaving ample space for flexibility, improvisation and infor-mality.[47] The principal patterns of interaction are self- and co-regulation, private-public partnerships, cooperative manage-ment and joint entrepreneurial ventures. Does this sound a bit confusing? Yes, indeed. Welcome to the world of networks, where nothing is simply top-down and imposed by a single 'enlightened' centre.

Two different galaxies

The existence of networks cannot be denied, but their role is often underplayed and presented as inferior to the role of states. States are seen as a superior historical formation that no network can match in terms of efficiency and legitimacy.

Networks can perform useful functions, it is conceded, but only if steered and aided by states. 'Networks are generally nested in hierarchies,' argued Paul Hirst, and if they act on their own, chaos and anarchy prevail. As Niall Ferguson put it: 'Trusting in networks to run the world is a recipe for anarchy: at best, power ends up in the hands of the Illuminati, but more likely it ends up in the hands of the Jacobins. Some today are tempted to give at least "two cheers for anarchism".'[48]

I find these views rather biased. Networks exist in parallel to states, sometimes acting as agents of states, and sometimes steering states in directions they initially resisted. Imperial and failed states have an impressive record of causing anarchy, for which networks can hardly be blamed. It is enough to study the history of Syria or Afghanistan to see state-induced chaos. The Russian invasion of Ukraine also triggered chaos, and networks, together with states, tried to reduce the damage.[49] Besides, the point is not to judge whether states or networks are running the world. The point is to understand the difference between the world of states and the world of networks. It is also to see how states and networks can act in synergy, and by the same token enhance the quality of global, national and local governance. How can this be accomplished?

First, we need to change our mental maps, which see states at the centre of the political universe with networks as tiny unidentified objects circulating around. Anne-Marie Slaughter has described it nicely:

Think of a standard map of the world, such as might have hung in your fifth-grade classroom, showing the borders and capitals of all the countries. That is a chessboard view. Now think of a map of the world at night, with the lit-up bursts of cities and highly concentrated regions and the dark swaths of rural areas and wilderness. Those corridors of light mark roads, cars, houses, and offices; they mark the networks of human relationships where families and workers and travellers come together. That is the web view. It is a map not of separation, marking off boundaries of sovereign power, but of connection, of the density and intensity of ties across boundaries.[50]

You may ask yourself, which map of the world is more real? Would you rather live in the world of networks or states? The answer is anything but simple. Both of these maps are real; and most of us are already living in both worlds. The problem is that only states enjoy formal powers over public decisions, although these powers are often more apparent than real, I must add.

States and networks view power differently, however, and they practise politics differently. This often creates tensions and misunderstandings. To start with, there is a tension between territorially bounded states claiming exclusive sovereignty, and unbounded networks ignoring sovereignty claims. Networks often assume a prominent role in cases of state failure because there is a power vacuum, which they can fill in without challenging states. The Georgian Orthodox Church, mentioned earlier, rose to 'diplomatic' prominence because relations between Georgia and Russia had completely broken down following violent clashes in 2008. State failure also gives way to the prominent role of humanitarian NGOs in bringing relief to people suffering from hunger or a lack of housing. In situations where there is no crisis, most states guard their upper hand, and view their relations with networks as between a principal and an agent. In other words, only states are invited to sit at the dinner table, while networks are graciously allowed to wash the dishes afterwards.

For instance, the 2016 Pact of Amsterdam signed by EU member states recognized the role of cities in tackling (state-made) problems such as poverty, air pollution or joblessness, but it failed to grant cities direct access to relevant decisions and resources.[51] In 2021 the UN Secretary-General, António Guterres, outlined his vision of a 'more networked and inclusive multilateral system', able to leverage 'the capabilities of non-state actors to deliver global public goods and manage the risks of an interconnected world'. However, the states which control the United Nations have shown little intention of helping him realize this vision.[52]

Why do states and networks hardly ever openly clash regarding uneven access to decisions and resources? Are networks scared to challenge all-powerful states? I do not think so. Networks simply play a different power game than states. States view power as capability amounting to mostly material strength, measured in hardware (arms) and treasure (gross domestic product). Networks may well enjoy posh offices and money, but they view power as relational; the stronger the quality and density of the ties you enjoy, the more power you possess. States are jealous of their borders and right to rule within these borders. Networks are more interested in problem-solving within or across state borders with no claim to exclusive authority; they do not challenge hierarchies because they are more interested in loose lateral arrangements that attract investment, generate technological innovation and promote cultural exchanges.[53] States value clear rules, institutional commitments and strong chains of command, while networks value speed, flexibility, adaptability and the possibility of an exit. States chiefly fear the loss of sovereignty, while networks fear being cut off from communication channels and information.

However, there are also situations in which states and networks find themselves face to face, flagging opposing solutions to specific matters. Networks usually prefer decentralized and differentiated answers to the problems they tackle, while states tend to prefer uniform and centrally directed solutions. Networks are more relaxed than states about free-riding and prefer to rely on self-policing and overlapping checking mechanisms to assure coordination. Policies are legitimate for states if they reflect the agreed procedures, while for networks policies are legitimate if they are inclusive and trust-based. Of course, these are general statements that do not apply uniformly to all networks or states, but they help us to understand the difference between these two galaxies and identify possible clashes and fields of cooperation.

States may well be in charge of the existing institutional structures, but digital technology clearly empowers networks more than states.[54] First, the internet has enlarged the scope of connectivity and communication beyond state borders. Efforts to contain connectivity and communication within state borders are probably futile and certainly costly. When the Kremlin blocked access to Facebook and Twitter in March 2022, Russians moved communication to their own digital messaging application Telegram, with servers outside Russia, and even utilized dating sites to continue informal exchanges unabated.[55] Second, the scale of connectivity and communication is also enlarged by the internet; the enormous volume of transactions and content on the internet far exceeds the capacity of states to control it. Facebook, the most used online social network worldwide, has circa 2.93 billion monthly active users.[56] Telegram has a global user base of at least 500 million. Third, the internet has allowed the existing institutions to operate on a different scale and timeframe than those run by states. Transformed or new institutions usually resemble networks and they are vaguely aligned with state structures. Finally, the internet changes the polity; public discourse, collaboration and direct action are now chiefly taking place through the internet where simple notions of family, religion, class and nation have to compete with numerous hybrid identities and loyalties.

We may conclude that time is on the side of networks, with states gradually fading away. In my view, such a conclusion would be premature, if not dangerous. The point is not to get rid of states, but to make states work in tandem with networks. Can this be done properly?

Living in a networked world

It has been suggested that humans are moving into the digital space because life in the physical space is so disappointing. The same reflection does not necessarily apply to states and networks. Some of those who are currently unhappy with the performance of nation-states do not want to dump them and embrace networks. They are proud to honour their national flags, borders and soldiers, and they detest the world of networks with fuzzy borders, multiple identities and confusing chains of command. These people trust only those who speak their language and they elect politicians who make them proud of their respective country. Can a network, especially a digital one, be called home or *heimat*? To whom can we address our political grievances in a network? How can transparency and accountability work in the complex, even mysterious world of networks? Citizens may well be part of numerous networks, but they still want their states back, don't they?

The loudest calls for the re-creation of strong, sovereign and proud nation-states come from nativists and autocrats, and their aggressive language makes me nervous. However, it is not only extreme-right demagogues who want their states back. The prospect of a virtual state run by networks is not appealing to moderate citizens either.[57] They fear that moving from the system of states to a mysterious system of networks will deprive them of tangible juridical, social and even physical protection. Is a viable social policy conceivable without a strong state? They fear swapping imperfect national democracy for a mysterious system of networks where unidentifiable and unaccountable actors behave selfishly with no oversight, let alone punishment. Are there any encouraging examples of democracy working beyond nation-states? 'Without a state, no modern democracy is possible,' declared two gurus of democratic studies, Linz and Stepan.[58] Ralf Dahrendorf added: 'Apart from nation-states, we shall never find appropriate institutions for democracy.'[59] Even the democracy practised by the European Union is opaque, to put it mildly.[60] Can the term democracy be applied to NGOs or firms, sceptics query?

These fears are legitimate, but they are often overblown, if not misguided. To start with, there is a growing body of literature suggesting that democracy cannot be confined to states only and focused exclusively on elections, parties and parliaments. I will elaborate on this in Chapter 8, but let me mention here that 'power scrutinizing and power checking mechanisms', exercised chiefly by networks, have gradually transformed 'the spirit, language, political geometry, and everyday dynamics of democracy'.[61] The notion (and *locus*) of democracy has never been static, but it evolved under the pressure of societal and technological developments.[62]

Moreover, and more to the point here, nobody proposes replacing states with networks. I just invite you to consider how to make the two work in harmony. Inviting some networks to the decision-making table should strengthen rather than weaken states. This is because the prime features of networks, such as speed, scale, enhanced communication and deliberation, can benefit global and regional governance. In fact, states accustomed to working with cities, NGOs and international bodies have proved stronger rather than weaker. Germany offers an excellent example. The transformation of the Ruhr region and the city of Essen from an environmentally devastated mining site into a service and financial centre with impressive green infrastructure was possible because the Federal German government understood the need to work together with local and European authorities.

The Ruhr is not the only place in Europe where important sectors such as energy, migration, environment, health and safety are handled by a variety of public and private actors on the local, regional, national and European levels. Cooperation is usually informal, voluntary and differently structured from case to case – but this does not undermine its significance. States may be formally in the driving seat but, in reality, they are dependent both on local authorities, such as cities, and transnational authorities, such as the EU or the UN, to effectively relocate migrants, address energy shortages or enforce food safety standards. Consider the case of the Randstad, a polycentric urban area in the western Netherlands, comprising Amsterdam, Rotterdam, The Hague, Utrecht and several smaller cities. This densely populated region does not even have its own distinct statistics, let alone a formal administrative identity – and yet, according to the OECD, it has developed into an advanced urban economy with many leading sectors, such as logistics, horticulture and financial services. The Randstad has one of the lowest unemployment rates when compared to OECD countries, and it is one of the most attractive metropolitan areas for foreign direct investment. Governance in the Randstad is multilevel, with urban, national and transnational authorities working hand in hand with NGOs and private firms. In sum, there are already numerous examples showing that states and networks can work together for the benefit of citizens. My aim is to advance, legitimize and formalize this practice.

Will networks dilute or even pervert democracy? Networks are certainly more informal, flexible and complex than states, but this does not necessarily mean that they are neither transparent nor accountable. Most networks are anything but secret, and they respect the law and their own codes of conduct. Some complex networks can escape formal democratic controls, but they are subject to a variety of informal controls that are less present in hierarchical systems. The dispersion of power contributes to accountability because different centres watch each other's moves and publicize abuses of power. The enhanced deliberation that characterizes networks also contributes to accountability because issues are considered in more depth by a variety of actors. True, national parliaments find it difficult to gain an insight into

the multicentred bargaining of networks, but this only underlines the growing inadequacy of traditional forms of democratic control. In other words, one should not idealize the
system of democratic accountability practised in nation-states.
Elections represent a very crude means of controlling officials.
Parliaments are under fire for failing to perform the necessary
controls, largely because they lack adequate expertise and
resources. This probably explains why less than 10 per cent
of people trust their parliaments in democracies such as the
United States and Lithuania, with similar trends evident in
the Arab world, East Asia and Pacific.[63] My point, again, is
not to discredit states, but to suggest that some networks
can be included in our governance system currently dominated by states. We can discuss which networks deserve to
have formal access to public decisions, but the idea that states
are legitimate actors by definition, while networks are some
mysterious if not suspicious political object, is at odds with
reality.[64]

Networks are joining hands with states, even in the fields
of defence and security that are perceived as the exclusive
domain of states. Today, national armies extensively rely on
private military contractors which operate like networks.[65]
Financial networks are crucial in undermining the enemy's
capacity to wage wars.[66] NGOs are helping to maintain
informal channels of communication between states formally
at war.[67] One can even argue that the soft power exercised by
networks is more effective in defeating autocrats than the hard

military power exercised by states.[68] Autocrats most fear their competitors' power to attract or seduce their own people, and this kind of power is exercised by the media, NGOs and artists who are part of the global liberal network.

If we invite networks to the decision-making table, will it not complicate governance and lead to anarchy? Is the notion of 'polycentric networked governance' not a mere buzzword with little practical application? Governance is indeed about the maintenance of the collective order, but there are various ways of achieving this. Unitary, centralized governance that

201

leaves little room for differentiation and flexibility has proved autocratic and ineffective numerous times in history. Anarchy is often caused by the incompetence of a government with no roots in society and out of sync with economic trends. Order can be enhanced by decentralization and differentiation that fosters consensus and brings decisions closer to the sites that are governed. Students of governance never tire of repeating that an effective system of governance must be able to represent the basic types of variety found in the system to be governed. The more diverse the qualities to be governed, the more diverse the necessary governing measures and structures, and the more diverse the relationship between them.[69]

These observations do not imply an endorsement of neoliberal free-riding; they are efforts to navigate the modern world with its complex vertical and horizontal connections, formal and informal.[70] As Mark Bevir from the University of California, Berkeley, put it:

> The state has become increasingly dependent on organizations in civil society and more constrained by international linkages. On the one hand, the public sector in many states has shifted away from bureaucratic hierarchy and toward markets and networks. On the other hand, states are increasingly tangled up in transnational and international settings as a result of the internationalization of industrial and financial transactions, the rise of regional blocs and growing concerns about global problems such as terrorism and the

environment. Governance here captures the formal and informal ways in which states have attempted to respond to the changing global order.[71]

Of course, a diversified, complex environment is not easy to steer. Negotiating with networks can be time – and energy – consuming, producing decentralized floating arrangements that are merely suboptimal if not vague.[72] However, governance specialists remind us that an effective system of governance does not need to be hierarchical and state-based. (And the concept of the state needs to be located socially, disaggregated institutionally and reorganized into its various component policy networks.)[73] An effective system of governance does not even need to be territorial, or territorially fixed. (And the concept of territorial governance need not entail mutual exclusion.) In stable, predictable conditions states can usually perform relatively well, but in a situation of crisis and instability, flexible, innovative and resilient networks can perform better than heavily bureaucratized and centralized states.

Order and anarchy are always relative, as are complexity and uncertainty. This is why in Helga Nowotny's study of the broken timelines and fragmented spaces caused by the internet, she coined the new concept of an 'orderly mess'.[74] Perhaps we need to adopt a novel way of ordering that does not see complexity and plurality as a threat. Perhaps we ought to liberate ourselves from the myths propagated by statists about the alleged virtues of hierarchical governance within fixed territorial borders. Statists usually have material stakes in maintaining the status quo, and they will paint each move to share state power and resources with other actors as leading to anarchy. There is no plausible reason to 'give three cheers' to that kind of statist quest for monopoly.

The fifth estate

The idea to grant some networks access to public decisions and resources does not amount to a revolution, but rather to filling the institutional vacuum created by successive unbounding revolutions – economic and digital, in particular. The densely networked environment of today requires new institutional structures and modes of governance. Some states have understood this already and have begun to work hand in hand with local and transnational actors on a daily basis. These practices need to spread and evolve into durable, transparent and publicly accepted arrangements. Failure to do this will represent futile efforts to turn back the clock of history. Numerous networks already form a fifth pillar of democracy, next to the courts, parliaments, the civil service and the media. They have the unique ability to frame and steer political issues by generating ideas, sharing information and advocating for alternative solutions to solving problems.[75]

The failure to embrace change will also assist those nativist politicians promising to make their states 'great again' by central-izing power and ruling at their whim. Poland and Hungary have vividly demonstrated the dangers of such nostalgic, statist politics. The return of the proud and sovereign state in Budapest and Warsaw, enacted by the ruling parties, amounts to cutting the funds of cities run by mayors from opposition parties, persecuting NGOs that refuse to embrace government policies and micro-managing public media, museums, hospitals, schools and universities. All this is done in the name of the Polish and Hungarian state.

It is time for states to open themselves up and admit other actors to the decision-making table. States must adopt certain forms of networked governance, and networks, in turn, must accept regulation that is more stringent. The challenge is not so much to design new institutions (for instance, the European Parliament could create a second chamber featuring cities, regions and NGOs; within the United Nations the status of NGOs could be upgraded). Rather, the challenge is to find a new balance between local and global concerns, between the requirements of coordination and deliberation, and between quick solutions to urgent problems and long-term investments and engagements. Most studies on governance concentrate on managerial or legal ways of bridging the gap between states and networks. Yet behind states and networks are real people with conflicting ideologies and material interests. Those supporting denationalized liberalism clash with those supporting networked nationalism; supporters of global governmentality are at odds with cyber reactionaries.[76] Moreover, networks are by nature more fluid and informal than traditional institutions such as courts or parliaments. Soft laws are therefore better suited to regulating networks than hard laws.[77] Diversified and flexible governing arrangements are more suited for networks than rigid, centralized and hierarchical ones.

The question is what to do with unlawful networks and with pathologies associated with networks operating on the web. My answer is simple: threats created by criminal networks demand coordinated, networked responses by states and legitimate networks. The latter understand better than states how illicit networks operate, they often know informal communities better than states, and they are savvy users of the internet. Even resourceful states have proved sluggish and clumsy in adjusting to the digital revolution, and could benefit from external help. As a group of distinguished academics put it: 'Governments have been slow and inefficient in taking advantage of the internet . . . as information technology became increasingly networked and interactive, bureaucratic culture in large states in particular mounted considerable barriers to innovation.'[78] It has proved particularly hard for states to regulate the internet single-handedly in a traditional top-down, territory-bounded manner. The internet can only be steered properly through 'multi-stake-holder processes' relying on the cooperation of networks.[79]

Of course, it takes two to tango. If networks utilize the digital space, they should also make sure that this space is safe and accessible to everybody. They should join hands with states to prevent cyber-crimes, digital monopolies and the proliferation of AI-enabled lethal robots and drones.[80]

Despotic states are likely to insist on their sovereign rights to defend phony notions of national interests.[81] They should therefore be put under pressure by citizens organized in networks below and above the space occupied by these states. As John Keane showed very well, even despotic rulers fear the power of networks able to mobilize on and off line:

> Digital mutinies and nonviolent strikes by organized groups can give birth to a rebellious civil society . . . Backed by demands for public accountability and supported by networked civil society actions and citizens' organizations, the push for monitory democracy can spread, even across borders, into the heartlands of despotic states.[82]

In democracies we can hopefully settle differences and conflicts peacefully, but the changes recommended in this chapter will not happen by themselves. Have you made a donation lately to your favourite NGO? Have you joined any of the civic initiatives launched by your local government? Did you take part in national elections? If enough of us answer positively to these questions, then despotism does not need to be the future of democracy in the age of networks.

8

RENEWING THE COSMOPOLIS

I wrote this book in Venice, a city that has practised the politics of time and space for over a thousand years. Medieval Venice was, in essence, a multicultural global city. This global city inspired my notion of Cosmopolis. Marco Polo, an early protagonist of what we now call globalization, was born in Venice in 1254. His Venice was a master in expanding its spatial reach to remote places such as Mombasa, Muscat, Calcutta, Malacca and Guangzhou. It also controlled some Crimean city ports and fought wars over them, not with the Russian but with the Ottoman Empire.

Medieval Venice also practised the politics of bounded space. The first ghetto was instituted in Venice in 1516, when Jews were forced to live in a segregated area of the city. The politics of time was also practised in the Venetian ghetto as Jews were obliged to reside within the restricted area during the night. The gates to the ghetto were opened in the morning at the ringing of the *marangona*, the famous Venetian bell (*campanile*) in St Mark's Square, and locked in the evening. Permanent, round-the-clock surveillance of the gates was put in place at the Jewish residents' expense. A splendid public clock on the Moors Tower, situated next to the *campanile*, was Venice's symbol of political and religious power from 1499. As David Rooney has accurately observed: 'With clocks, the elites wield power, make money, govern citizens and control lives.'[1]

This book was also written during the Covid-19 pandemic and, naturally, all its intrusions into our space and time influenced my perspective. Venice is a place most used to pandemics. The now popular term 'quarantine' was coined in Venice during one of the gravest plagues, the so-called Black Death of the fourteenth century that originated in China and killed some 25 million Europeans. The Venetian term *quarantena* implied a forty-day restriction on the movement of people, animals and goods, imposed to prevent the spread of disease or pests.

Venice is also an inspiring place to write about a politics that is not only confined to nation-states. The Republic of Venice was created in AD 697 and existed for 1,100 years – something that contemporary nation-states can only aspire to. *La Serenissima*, which in English means the Most Serene Republic (of Venice), resembled contemporary republics in name only. It was a portal city-state with a truly global network of trade, art and politics. The Republic was ruled by the Doge, elected by members of the Great Council of Venice. Venice's enormous wealth was rooted not only in maritime trade, but also in an effective system of governance, sound legal framework and well-equipped army and navy. Even today, Venice's relations with the Italian state are complicated, to put it mildly. During the recent pandemic, the President of the Veneto Region, Luca Zaia, frequently questioned or even defied the instructions coming from the national government in Rome. In 1997, a group of armed Venetian separatists occupied the *campanile* and proclaimed (in vain) the independence of *Il Veneto*.

You may say that I found myself in the perfect place at the perfect time to write this particular book. The term 'perfect' may sound ironic, however. This is because Venice was hit particularly hard by the deadly virus, and I was confined to the small space of my flat for several long months. I could only continue my work thanks to the much-criticized internet and internet providers such as BT or Tim, among others. This probably explains why I refrained from demonizing them in the previous chapter, rightly or wrongly.

Identifying problems

This book started with the bold statement that the world is confronted with grave problems that go beyond Covid-19. Problems, however grave, do not necessarily represent a serious threat, provided that we are able to cope with them effectively. Sadly, this seems to no longer be the case because democratic politics is not suited for handling time and space in a way that safeguards the interests of future generations and overcomes state borders. The pages that followed tried to substantiate this claim by showing how political actors try, but fail, to safeguard our future.

The historical perspective adopted in this book highlights an interesting paradox. We may now have a greater array of technological and institutional means at our disposal than ever before to command time and space, but we misuse these sophisticated means, causing more damage to the world than good. For instance, the advanced form of 'turbo-capitalism' is generating huge profits, but chiefly for the famous or infamous 1 per cent. It is also damaging our natural environment beyond repair, disregarding basic workers' rights and generating conflicts within and across state borders. Markets are no longer under democratic scrutiny, and they have managed to impose a ceaseless 24/7 economy upon us, operating across individual polities with little regard for their distinct social contracts. Besides, in a 'turbo-capitalism' of cascading inequalities, it is hard to form any social contract, and hence competing egoisms thrive. These competing egoisms generated by inequality within and across state borders have also made it difficult to arrive at a commonly shared definition of minimal rights to space and time.

Another telling example concerns the digital technology that has compressed time and space to a degree unknown in the past. The military-industrial sector was first to utilize this technology for modern warfare rather than for combating ecological threats. Autocratic states have proved skilful in applying digital technology for the mass surveillance of citizens, while e-democracy is still rudimental in liberal states. Organized crime penetrates the internet, while hospitals and schools in large parts of the world lack modern computers and a Wi-Fi connection. The spreading of smears and post-truth is pronounced on social (digital) platforms, while the defenders of science and facts dominate primarily the old media. It looks like 'bad guys' operate in cyberspace more effectively than the 'good guys'. This means that the spread of digital technology and AI is not benefiting the world satisfactorily.

I have established that nation-states that are supposed to govern the public sphere for the benefit of citizens (and not just power- or share-holders) are unable to live up to their promises, let alone expectations. Moreover, states protect the partisan interests of their own national electorates, undermining solutions for which a concerted international involvement is indispensable. Of course, some states are more impotent and/or selfish than others. Moreover, it matters who is in charge of a given state. The United States has been governed very differently by Presidents Obama, Trump and Biden. The Brazil led by President Bolsonaro and the Brazil of President Lula da Silva look in many respects like two different states.

Despite all these differences and nuances, we can observe that even robust and well-governed states such as Germany tend to privilege the electorate of the day at the expense of

212

future generations. Germany's commitment to international causes is not without limits, and nor is its solidarity towards less fortunate states such as Greece, for instance.[2] President Biden's difficulties in satisfying American and international public opinion show that even a drastic change of leadership cannot produce wonders because of the structural conditions within which states operate. When power is exclusively in the hands of sovereign states defending their territorial prerogatives, it is hard to think about a world resembling a multicultural global city inhabited by people who respect each other and try to save the planet; in other words, a Cosmopolis.

Myopic and territory-bound democracy can hardly generate a common global political will. If firms are

transnational, and parliaments are national, laws are always inadequate. Some years ago, it was hoped that ideology, in the form of liberal internationalism, would guide and bind the world, but this proved to be naive.[3] Today, despotic states feel free to act at their will and one democracy after another is confronted by their own illiberal demagogues. Some of us seem resigned, others voice their protest, yet others think that this is not for real, and there will soon be a happy ending, like in Hollywood movies.

In the past, humans have demonstrated incredible intelligence, and the willpower to survive against all odds. Not everybody was lucky, but those who survived tried to better prepare for the next catastrophe. The Universal Declaration of Human Rights by the United Nations was one such notable response to man-made catastrophes. Today, the UN has offices in 193 countries, and employs 37,000 people, but the effects of its work are grossly inadequate. Human rights are openly being questioned even in self-proclaimed democratic states, not to mention autocracies with or without a seat at the UN Security Council. The European Union was created to put the ghosts of nationalism to rest and seven decades later we observe a remarkable resurgence of ugly nationalism across the continent. Clearly, something has gone wrong with these noble projects, which are possibly broken beyond repair.[4] Can we regain control over the roller-coaster? Can we create public institutions able to master time and space for the benefit of many, not just a few? How will the world look without a future?

Hope and despair

In the book *The World without a Future* by the American writer Nazarea Andrews, infected zombies begin to roam the world, destroying everything in their path and decimating the human population. This is how we often think about epochal crises: they are like a huge and mysterious power that we cannot control. A more realistic vision of human demise is presented by Alfonso Cuarón's film *Children of Men* (2006). Here, a deadly virus also plays an important role, but some of the destructive forces are clearly man-made. There is an authoritarian state spying on its citizens and demonizing migrants. There is also an important economic factor. 'No one can escape the ordinary unhappiness of capitalist realism', writes Gavin Jacobson in his review of the film in the *New Statesman*, 'endless forms, long commutes, idle queues, crowded streets, and trying to convince your boss to let you work from home.'[5] The combination of Covid-19, neoliberal economics and nativist politics makes this version of the apocalypse strikingly familiar and frightening. The Russian threat of nuclear strike has stimulated commentators to talk about another kind of total destruction.[6]

However, we can also imagine a softer version of the world without a future; we can call this a benign-neglect scenario with rather malign implications. Under this scenario, destruction comes gradually, by default, and largely in disguise. States are visibly still in charge, but they are failing to solve domestic and international problems; democracy is formally in place, but it hardly generates any legitimacy for political leaders; stock markets are going up, but inequalities and poverty continue to grow. Under this scenario, populist politicians pretend to act as statesmen, and liberal politicians pretend to listen to the people. Employers pretend to offer decent pay, and employees pretend to work efficiently. International organizations engage in multiple projects, and make reassuring declarations, but climate change, migration and violent conflicts progress unabated. Citizens are cynical, atomized and unable to form a common front for anything constructive. They simply 'normalize' and tolerate the already pronounced 'apocalypse', to use Srećko Horvat's words.[7]

Some years before the fall of Communism in Eastern Europe, I experienced a similar kind of situation. The regime could neither satisfy citizens, nor force them into obedience. Our leaders had no vision, and we had no hope. The political and economic system was like a colossus on shaky pillars. Civil society was like a maze: diversified, dispersed and alienated. We called it *Absurdistan* at the time, and a book by Tadeusz Konwicki entitled *A Minor Apocalypse* perfectly reflects the bizarre atmosphere of this period. 'But in all that suffering, the most painful suffering of all was the consciousness that it was banal,' observed Konwicki. 'Our epoch is that of noble doubts, blessed uncertainty, sacred hypersensitivity, divine wishy-washiness.'[8] Konwicki's book was a colourful satire, but it left the reader with a sense of despair and bitterness. And then, in the 1980s, things suddenly changed. People started to engage in collective action across the entirety of Eastern

Europe. Intellectuals started to envisage alternative futures. Wise leaders suddenly emerged, not just among the democratic opposition, but even in the Kremlin. Think of Mikhail Gorbachev and his advisers such as Andrei Grachev, a frequent visitor to my college in Oxford.[9]

This personal history has made me think that there is always hope amid gloom and misery. Problems will not simply go away, but there is no need to endorse an extreme pessimism that scares and paralyses citizens. We can reclaim our collective future and make politics work in sync with space and time. However, we need to be alert, imaginative, determined, and act with solidarity. Perhaps the shock caused by Covid-19 will come to be recognized as a historic wake-up call. It has shown us that humans are a vulnerable part of the vast biosphere. It has made us realize that the equilibrium we reached with our respective political classes in the twentieth century no longer stands in the twenty-first century. Perhaps the Russian invasion of Ukraine will make us realize that we cannot sacrifice freedom, disarmament and sustainable development on the altar of short-term economic gains unequally divided. Today, more than ever, we see an explosive mixture of technologically compressed time and space, weak transnational governance and a rebellious public with no clear lines of solidarity. The ensuing chaos is not only preventing timely responses to global challenges but also facilitating predatory behaviour by boorish firms and states, as well as ordinary criminals. If we indeed start to appreciate the sorry state of global affairs, we can try to do something about it. Where do we start?

Searching for remedies

Right now, you probably expect me to propose some tangible solutions to the problems identified. I will comply with this expectation, but half-heartedly. Half-heartedly, because most problems cannot be fixed by a handy repertoire of measures. Have you ever lost weight by reading books suggesting 'three easy steps' to lose 3 pounds a week? Or have you boosted your fortunes by following a manual on 'six proven ways to get rich quickly'? And yet you are perhaps expecting me to offer ready-made solutions for meeting not just personal objectives but also collective ones such as making war obsolete, the economy sustainable, democracy legitimate and society resilient to forthcoming catastrophes. I hope that the preceding chapters have made it clear that we are not likely to get a grip over time and space by adopting a handful of new decrees and managerial tricks.

Of course, simple solutions to complicated problems are not necessarily wrong. Inheritance tax is not going to eradicate inequality, but it could alleviate it to some extent. Solar energy does not represent a panacea for climate change, but it is better to heat houses with solar panels than with coal or oil. Even ambitious solutions such as a universal income or social housing will have only a limited impact. One implication of universal income is that we wouldn't need to 'sell' our time in order to survive, while social housing could offer shelter to penniless citizens. However, none of these measures would offer a comprehensive solution for handling time and space for the benefit of the planet and its citizens, current and future.

Complex problems require new regulations, budgets and technologies, as well as new economic, political and cultural structures and atmospheres. It is easier to introduce a different system of unemployment benefits than to change the public perception of social justice. Intergenerational politics is not just a function of economics or law, but also of family ties. War is not only about military capabilities, but also economic greed, historical fear and human error. Most of these factors can hardly be 'squeezed' into fancy figures and graphs. Nor is it enough to put them into electoral manifestos.

This brings me back to the issues of democracy and governance, which represent institutional solutions for doing politics in the liberal part of the world. These institutions are not supposed to be about a particular leader, party or ideology. Nor are they about a specific political blueprint for a desired Cosmopolis. They are about channelling competition and mitigating conflicts between leaders and ideas; about involving ordinary people in the process of decision-making; about selecting policies that are not only responsive but also effective. At present, democracy and governance are located chiefly in nation-states and this, in my view, hampers our ability to handle time and space. Democratic nation-states are, by their nature, interested in defending their own limited territory and they privilege their current, not prospective, voters. This in-built double institutional selfishness makes it difficult to address the transnational challenges that are dominant at present, and it also hampers future-oriented engagements. So, if we want to handle time and space better, we need to abolish the virtual monopoly of states on policy-making. Cosmopolitan democracy used to be seen as an optimal remedy for overcoming national selfishness. However, it proved to be a myth, not only because it underplayed the importance of national identities but also because it promised to move decisions to the global centre that is – by its nature – further away from ordinary people and from the problems to be tackled. We need to divide and spread power to make us more responsive and effective, depending on the context and issue. As the old saying goes: don't put all your eggs in one basket.

The emphasis on the process rather than the outcome of democratic policy-making is inspired by the writings of Hannah Arendt, Isaiah Berlin and Karl Popper.[10] For them the *process* of arriving at the future destination was as important as the final destination itself. They urged us to move forward through public reasoning, deliberation and bargaining, not by imposition, let alone force. Deliberation and bargaining do not need to be confined to nation-states only. Local and transnational actors should be empowered to play their essential part in policy-making because they speak for different constituencies and offer different time perspectives.

There are no 'obvious' answers to most questions confronting our planet and societies. Does nuclear energy represent a way out of the environmental crisis or a way to magnify this disaster? Is speed a threat or salvation for democracy? Do open borders undermine or secure our welfare? Not only politicians but also scientists are divided in answering these questions. What is good for the planet and humanity should not be decided by a handful of leaders in charge of the most powerful states. We need more open, flexible and responsive institutional arrangements to cope with an ever more interconnected world running at an ever higher speed.

Uncertainty in matters of time and space and the unintended consequences of human action also present arguments for dividing rather than concentrating power and for avoiding overly strategic visions, let alone utopia. Our ability to master the planet is limited, confronted with ambiguities and pregnant with dangers, not just opportunities. As John Dewey argued a century ago, indeterminacy in human affairs is double-edged: it can bring good things as well as bad, 'evil or . . . good fortune'.[11] This means that the future is likely to be hazy and only partly under our control, but this should not make us nervous. I grew up in Communist Europe where governments aspired to control everything in order to implement ambitious long-term plans, albeit with minimal results and little public enthusiasm. Besides, as Hartmut Rosa has pointed out: 'Where "everything is under control", the world no longer has anything to say to us, and where it has become newly uncontrollable, we can no longer hear it, because we cannot reach it.'[12]

The destination point for Popper and his disciples is an 'open society' guided by values such as liberty and equality,

REPAIRS

tolerance and anti-racism, the rule of law and accountable power, sustainable development, fair trade and peace. It is easier to preach than to realize these values, and some of them may be in conflict. For instance, equality demands curbs on property speculation in large cities, but developers see this as an assault on their economic freedom. Placing all our bets on liberty does not solve our problems, because liberty is a pluralistic concept. Is freedom of information or the right to privacy more important? Nevertheless, values represent a compass on the way to my desired Cosmopolis, however hazy. Science helps me to distinguish the difference between facts and gossip. The rest is up for grabs in a fair and transparent process of political bargaining.

Of course, I know that politics is seldom fair and transparent, but this is not an 'all or nothing' game as seen by dogmatic revolutionaries. I am aware that the capitalist hegemony over time and space will not be curbed by environmental or demographic pressures alone. We will need to stand up for our rights as employees, consumers and citizens. Yet I believe that institutions and governance systems can be reformed if we establish some priorities and exert adequate pressure.

By now, you already know my priorities. I propose moving beyond the primacy of nation-states and empowering other public actors at the local and transnational level. We should, in essence, move from a system governed by states to a system governed by networks. Networks are not just mysterious devices within our computers: urban, financial and social networks have already been shaping our daily lives for some time, although we struggle to find a proper vocabulary to talk about them. New, experimentalist forms of governance replacing traditional state structures are already practised in various forms around the world. Chapter 7 has discussed some of them, highlighting their unique assets, such as speed, flexibility and adaptability. Civic participation can be enhanced rather than curbed by embracing a networked governance.

The challenge is to make the shift from states to networks popular, durable and legally binding. Only in this way can it become an alternative to national politicians who promise to make their countries great by centralizing power and ruling by decree. The challenge is also to avoid the danger of creating various 'authority holes', leaving certain firms and citizens without jurisdiction and protection. Networks cannot act as 'floating islands' (*îles flottantes*) operating above the law and free from any coordination and supervision. Therefore, the new system led by networks needs to be accountable, transparent and institutionalized. Can this be accomplished?

Reclaiming the future

Most experts agree that networks are 'smooth operators' across time and space, but they struggle to see how governance by networks can be made democratic. Much depends on what we mean by democracy. If we mean a system in which citizens freely elect their representatives to a sovereign parliament, then we indeed have a problem. I do not think that one single parliament will ever be in charge of the world. The Global Parliament of Mayors is a terrific initiative, but it cannot aspire to represent all citizens of the world.[13] This applies even more to the Parliament of the World Religions.[14] The idea to create a United Nations' Parliamentary Assembly has been launched a few times in history with no success.[15] Even the European Parliament is opaque to some degree, although it envisages direct parliamentary elections every five years. The European Parliament does not have a governing cabinet or a governing programme to sustain or oppose. The powers of European Parliaments have increased over the years, but member states represented in the Council are key legislators within the EU, nevertheless. And I am not even talking about the absence of a

European or global *demos* important for the creation of genuine, transnational parliamentary representation.

However, the idea that democracy can only be located in nation-states and based on parliamentary representation is narrow, in my view. Historically, the notion of democracy has evolved in response to material and ideological pressures. Initially, democracy was confined to city-states such as Athens, and when cities encountered troubles governing beyond their walls, democracy did not die but was transferred to a larger unit better suited to cope with these pressures: the nation-state.[16] Democracy as such has also changed in this process; it became a representative democracy rather than an assembly democracy at the level of the city-state. Representative democracy has also undergone regular adjustments. On the eve of the twentieth century many parliamentary governments were still dependent on their local monarchs, elections were hardly free and electoral rights were severely restricted. In France and Belgium women were allowed to vote only after the Second World War. Today, not only nation-states, but also the system of parliamentary representation is in trouble.[17] Perhaps we need to locate democracy on levels above and below nation-states. Perhaps democracy does not only need to rely on representation, but also on citizens' participation, deliberation and contestation. Perhaps dispersing power between different territorial actors will make democracy more effective and legitimate.

Nation-states that see themselves as the sole democratic unit have lost or given up control over transnational economic, security, migratory and communicative flows. Stakeholders' communities correspond to national borders less and less. Powerful transnational actors, public and private, operate in the shadow of national democratic laws with little transparency and accountability. These days those who hold power are being better scrutinized by NGOs, digital media and think-tanks than by national parliaments. This is why I argued in the previous chapter that many networks possess a crucial controlling power, next to the courts, the media, the civil service and parliaments. Networks have the unique ability to generate and share information revealing the misconduct or negligence of those in charge of formal decision-making processes. They are, in essence, the fifth pillar or estate on which contemporary politics rests.

These developments cannot but influence the very notion of democracy. According to John Keane, democracy is no longer about delegating power to elected officials within confined territorial states. In the highly interdependent and high-speed environment of today, democracy is about self-governed networks monitoring traditional political institutions and forcing them to change their agendas, effectively breaking long-standing corporatist arrangements. 'Whether in the field of local, national or supranational government, or in the world of business and other NGOs and networks,' argues Keane, 'people and organizations that exercise power are now routinely subject to public monitoring and public contestation by an assortment of extra-parliamentary bodies.'[18]

If we agree that democracy does not need to be tied to territorially bounded nation-states, then numerous alternative institutional options emerge. Consider two diverse examples of sharing decision-making powers between different actors. The first, global, example is exemplified by the International Labour Organization (ILO), which received the Nobel Peace Prize for 'reducing injustice and contributing to peace' by creating international legislation improving the working conditions and social rights of employees.[19] The ILO has a unique, tripartite decision-making structure that brings together governments, employers and workers from all over the world. National governments are not the ILO's only masters, as is the case with other UN agencies.

The second, local, example is exemplified by the municipal council of Barcelona where elected officials share powers with ordinary citizens. Proposals suggested directly by citizens form 70 per cent of the agenda of the city administration.[20] Citizens are also able to monitor the implementation of each of their proposals, creating pressure on local authorities to reflect the agreed measures. Moreover, the recently created 'participatory budget' of Barcelona allows citizens to decide directly how millions of euros are spent for their neighbourhood.[21]

Similar hybrid democratic arrangements could proliferate throughout the world. For instance, the European Parliament could create a second chamber with representatives of cities, regions and NGOs. Speakers at World Climate Summits could be selected by environmental NGOs and not the hosting governments. The auditing of climate pledges could also be performed by NGOs, with states obliged to provide them with all the relevant information. With a little dose of fantasy, we can multiply analogous proposals.[22]

Friends of nation-states will not accept these arguments and will try to reverse the clock of history. They will insist that democracy, however flawed, can exist only in states, and they will oppose any democratic experiments. They will argue that states are the only guarantors of order, while networks are agents of anarchy. They will rubbish transnational organizations such as the European Union, or treat local authorities with disdain. They will ridicule 'people from anywhere' and punish those who destroy national monuments or burn national flags. Yet states are prone to change and decay. As are all human creations. Moving from the system of states to a system of networks is not the end of history. To cite Tadeusz Konwicki once again, 'The world can't die. Many generations have thought the world was dying. But it was only their world which was dying.'[23]

My vision of Cosmopolis does not envisage the disappearance of states, but it demands that states share power and resources with other public actors, local and transnational. Nor is my vision of Cosmopolis a blind endorsement of globalization – but I do oppose the current politics of restoring borders, driven by nativism and xenophobia. My vision of Cosmopolis does not advocate that all powers are transferred to networks, but it encourages moves to make governance more pluralistic, flexible and respectful of future generations. Time and space ought to be handled better than is the case at present. Democracy does not need to be myopic and confined to bordered space. It must be able to handle high speeds and overcome excessive presentism. Let's push for change and move forward through trial and error. I would rather make errors than allow the further destruction of our health, work, communities, neighbourhoods and biosphere. As T.S. Eliot reminded us in 'East Coker', trying is what we can and must do. In the dire circumstances of today, benign neglect would amount to a crime.[24]

ENDNOTES

PREFACE

1. See the Bertelsmann Stiftung transformation index available at BTI 2022 (bti-project.org). Sheri Berman offered an insighful historical overview of the interplay between democracy and autocracy. See Sheri Berman, *Democracy and Dictatorship in Europe: From the Ancien Régime to the Present Day*, Oxford University Press, New York, 2019.
2. Bruno Latour, *After Lockdown: A Metamorphosis*, Polity Press, Cambridge, 2021, p. 45.

1 IN SEARCH OF THE LOST FUTURE

1. Bruce Stokes, 'Public divided on prospects for the next generation', Pew Research Center, 2017. The outlook has turned even gloomier since then. See Michelle Fox, 'A majority of Americans think kids will be financially worse off than their parents, survey finds', cnbc.com, 2021.
2. EP Autumn 2021 Survey: Defending democracy: empowering citizens, https://europa.eu/eurobarometer/surveys/detail/2612; BBVA Foundation Study European Mindset, www.fbbva.es/wp-content/uploads/2017/05/dat/european_mindset_27042010.pdf.
3. Sam Shead. 'More than half of Europeans want to replace lawmakers with AI, survey says', www.cnbc.com/2021/05/27/europeans-want-to-replace-lawmakers-with-ai.html.
4. This comment concerns chiefly 38 most advanced states that are members of the Organisation for Economic Co-operation and Development (OECD). In non-OECD states such as China and India, millions were lifted out of poverty, although inequalities are also striking there. See Branco Milanovic, *Global Inequality: A New Approach for the Age of Globalization*, Belknap Press, Cambridge MA, 2018. Also Thomas Piketty, *The Economics of Inequality*, Belknap Press, Cambridge MA, 2015.

5. See for example George Eaton, 'Noam Chomsky: The world is at the most dangerous moment in human history', *New Statesman*, 17 September 2020, Gavin Jacobson, 'Yuval Noah Harari's 21 Lessons for the 21st Century is a banal and risible self-help book', *New Statesman*, 25 July 2021. For a historical overview of various visions of the decline and end of the world see Saul Friedlander, Gerard Holton, Leo Marx and Eugene Skolnikoff, eds, *Visions of Apocalypse: End or Rebirth?*, Holms & Meier, New York, 1985.

6. Steven Pinker, *The Better Angels of Our Nature: Why Violence Has Declined*, Penguin, London, 2011.

7. As a group of eight UN Foundation Next Generation Fellows put it in 2021: 'Today's young people are forced to confront crises that we did not cause. It is no wonder that we fear for our futures, and for the futures of our children and grandchildren.' United Nations Foundation, 'Next Generation Fellows. Our Future Agenda', Washington, DC, 2021, https://ourfutureagenda.org/report.

8. For pessimistic assessments on where capitalism and democracy are heading, see Wolfgang Streeck, *How Will Capitalism End?*, Verso, London, 2016, in particular p. 36. Also Niall Ferguson, *Doom: The Politics of Catastrophe*, Allen Lane, New York, 2021.

9. John Keane, 'Thoughts on Uncertainty', *Journal of Social and Political Philosophy*, 1/1, 2022, p. 3.

10. See for example Edward Luttwak, *Turbo-Capitalism: Winners and Losers in the Global Economy*, HarperCollins, New York, 1999. Also Naomi Klein, *The Shock Doctrine: The Rise of Disaster Capitalism*, Metropolitan Books, New York, 2006.

11. Recent studies of the Covid-19 pandemic indicate that measures of trust in the government and interpersonal trust, as well as less government corruption, had high statistically significant associations with lower standardized infection rates. High levels of government and interpersonal trust, as well as less government corruption, were also associated with higher Covid-19 vaccine coverage among middle-income and high-income countries where vaccine availability was more widespread. See Covid-19 National Preparedness Collaborators, 'Pandemic Preparedness and Covid-19: An Exploratory Analysis of Infection and Fatality Rates, and Contextual Factors Associated with Preparedness in 177 Countries, from Jan 1, 2020, to Sept 30, 2021', *The Lancet*, 399/10334, 16 April 2022, pp. 1489–512.

12. Jonathan White, 'WhatsApp Europe?', Social Europe, https//socialeurope.eu/whatsapp-europe. See also Jonathan White, 'The De-institutionalization of Power beyond the State', *European Journal of International Relations*, 28/1, 2022, pp. 187–208.

13. Markus Becker, 'A new controversy erupts around Ursula von der Leyen's text messages', *Der Spiegel*, 12 November 2021. Also Peter Walker, 'Government work often done on WhatsApp during Covid, says top official, *Guardian*, 22 March 2022.

14. See for example Wojciech Sadurski, *A Pandemic of Populists*, Cambridge University Press, Cambridge, 2022; Michael S. Schmidt, *Donald Trump v. The United States: Inside the Struggle to Stop a President*, Random House, New York, 2020.

15. The term 'governance' is uncontroversial in management studies, but contentious in democratic studies because it allegedly serves to camouflage power relations and makes no reference to democratic subjects. Such an interpretation of this term seems to me unjust. Governance in its essence is about the maintenance of collective order, the achievement of collective goals, and the collective process of rule through which order and goals are sought. Democracy is very much about similar matters, although from a different angle. See Jan Kooiman, ed., *Modern Governance*, Sage, London, 1993; Mark Bevir, *Democratic Governance*, Princeton University Press, Princeton, NJ, 2010.

16. Bo Rothstein, *The Quality of Government: Corruption, Social Trust, and Inequality in International Perspective*, University of Chicago Press, Chicago, IL, 2011, pp. 77–97.

17. Marc Plattner, 'Reflections on "Governance"', *Journal of Democracy*, 24/4, 2013, pp. 23–7.

18. 'North Korean regime finally admits Kim Jong-un cannot magically bend time and space', *Daily Telegraph*, 22 May 2020.

19. I am using the typical Western notion of time and space, past and present, here and there, which may not be shared by, for example, indigenous people living in states such as Canada, New Zealand, Australia, Bolivia, Chile and Peru. See Chris Sinha, Vera da Silva Sinha, Jörg Zinken and Wany Sampaio, 'When Time Is Not Space: The Social and Linguistic Construction of Time Intervals and Temporal Event Relations in an Amazonian Culture', *Language and Cognition*, 3/1, 2011, pp. 137–69; May Yuan, Atsushi Nara and James Bothwell, 'Space–time Representation and Analytics', *Annals of GIS*, 20/1, 2014, pp. 1–9.

20. George W. Wallis, 'Chronopolitics: The Impact of Time Perspectives on the Dynamics of Change', *Social Forces*, 49/1, 1970, pp. 102–8.

21. Steve Henrix, 'On New Year's, our calendar's crazy history, and the switch that changed Washington's birthday', *Washington Post*, 31 December 2017.

22. Charles S. Maier, *Once within Borders: Territories of Power, Wealth, and Belonging since 1500*, Belknap Press, Cambridge, MA, 2016.

23. Jonathan White, *Politics of Last Resort: Governing by Emergency in the European Union*, Oxford University Press, Oxford, 2019. Also Giorgio Agamben, *State of Exception*, Chicago University Press, Chicago, IL, 2005.

24. Giuseppe Tomasi di Lampedusa, *The Leopard*, Pantheon, London, 1960, p. 319.

25. Andreas Schäfer and Wolfgang Merkel, 'The Temporal Constitution of Democracy', in *The Oxford Handbook of Time and Politics*, Klaus H. Goetz, ed., Oxford University Press, Oxford, 2019, p. 7. See also Dennis F. Thomson, 'Democracy in Time: Popular Sovereignty and Temporal Representation', *Constellation*, 2/12, 2005, pp. 245–61.

26. Jonathan Boston, 'Assessing the Options for Combatting Democratic Myopia and Safeguarding Long-term Interests', *Futures: The Journal of Policy, Planning and Futures Studies*, 125, 2021. Also Michael K. MacKenzie, 'Introduction', *The Democratic Myopia Thesis*, Oxford Academic, Oxford, 2021, pp. 3–26; Oxford Martin School, 'Now for the Long Term. Report of the Oxford Martin Commission for Future Generations', 2013.

27. Alexandria Symonds, 'Why don't young people vote?', *New York Times*, 8 October 2020.

28. David Willetts, *The Pinch: How the Baby Boomers Took their Children's Future – And Why They Should Give it Back*, Atlantic Books, London, 2010.
29. Stephan De Spiegeleire, Clarissa Skinner and Tim Sweijs, 'The rise of popular sovereignism: What it is, where it comes from and what it means for international security and defense', The Hague Centre for Strategic Studies, The Hague, 2017; Jan Zielonka, *Counter Revolution: Liberal Europe in Retreat*, Oxford University Press, Oxford, 2018, pp. 99–113.
30. Pierre Hassner, 'Beyond the Three Traditions: The Philosophy of War and Peace in Historical Perspective', *International Affairs*, 70/4, 1994, pp. 737–56; David Runciman, *Confronting Leviathan: A History of Ideas*, Profile Books, London, 2021.
31. Monica Duffy Toft, *The Geography of Ethnic Violence: Identity, Interests, and the Indivisibility of Territory*, Princeton University Press, Princeton, NJ, 2003, p. 256; Paul Hirst, *Space and Power: Politics, War and Architecture*, Polity Press, Cambridge, 2005, p. 272; Miles Kahler and Barbara F. Walter, *Territoriality and Conflict in an Era of Globalization*, Cambridge University Press, Cambridge, 2006, p. 340; and John A. Vasquez and Marie T. Henehan, *Territory, War, and Peace*, Routledge, New York, 2010.
32. See for example Jonathan Fenby, *Will China Dominate the 21st Century?*, Polity Press, Cambridge, 2014; Hal Brands and Jake Sullivan, 'China Has Two Paths to Global Domination', *Foreign Policy*, 22 May 2020; John Keane, *When Trees Fall, Monkeys Scatter: Rethinking Democracy in China*, World Scientific, Singapore, 2017.
33. The European Commission's initial handling of the vaccines has been widely criticized, also by myself, but vaccine nationalism proved counter-productive. See Jan Zielonka, 'Fünf Lektionen aus dem AstraZeneca-Debakel', Zeit Online, 2 February 2021; Sylvie Kauffmann, 'Europe's vaccine rollout has descended into chaos', *New York Times*, 4 February 2021.
34. We should not assume that policies of autocratic states are set in stone. China is seen as a traditional territorial state cherishing fixed borders with no intention to share sovereignty. However, traditional Chinese political thinking defined territory primarily in cultural terms. The Chinese world was one of hierarchy, with the Han civilization in the middle and the barbarians on the peripheries. Since there was constant intermingling and movement of populations, the exact location between centres and peripheries could not be established in linear terms. Such thinking can still be traced in contemporary China. Consider the relations between the Han and Uyghurs inhabiting 'the same land', but living in different 'parallel universes', to use Ruth Ingram's words. Moreover, a dense network linking the overseas Chinese with the mainland population makes it difficult to talk about a hard and fixed border. The border between China and Hong Kong and Taiwan is also fuzzier than envisaged by the Westphalian paradigm. The Chinese concept of time, as pointed out by Harold A. Innis, is plural and 'characterized by a succession of times, which reflects their social organization with its interest in hierarchy and relative stability, as well as their concept of space'. If one conceives contemporary China as a kind of empire, a different notion of space and time emerges. Empires often exercise territorial control through informal penetration and they share considerable powers with their respective peripheries in order to

avoid free-riding and rebellions. Confucius and his followers such as Mencius or Xunzi believed that differences could be maintained in harmony. Rather than arguing for imposing direct rule on the peripheries through force they believed China could help 'barbarians' to civilize themselves by the appeal of its universal culture and the attraction of its administrative model. Contemporary Chinese will admit that China has also a tradition that rests on force rather than benevolence. But 'legalism' imposing draconian laws by impersonal bureaucracy is ill-suited to the current age of globalization, they argue. This is why China has endorsed the concept of the 'harmonious world' based on respect for other actors and moral values. This may prove to be mere propaganda, but it may also be a sign of possible alternatives to President Xi's worldview. See Chen Zhimin, 'Confucius' Ideal of Peace in the Contemporary World', in *Diplomacy in Theory and Practice*, Karin Aggestam and Magnus Jerneck, eds, Liber, Malmö, 2009, pp. 58–73, and Xunwu Chen, 'A Rethinking of Confucian Rationality', *Journal of Chinese Philosophy*, 4, 2008, pp. 483–50. Also K.J. Holsti, *Taming the Sovereigns: Institutional Change in International Politics*, Cambridge University Press, Cambridge, 2004, p. 73; Ruth Ingram, 'The Uyghurs and the Han: 1 World, 2 Universes', *The Diplomat*, 4 October 2018; Harold A. Innis, *Changing Concepts of Time*, Rowman & Littlefield, Lanham, MD, 2004, p. 94; Jan Zielonka, 'Empires and the Modern International System', *Geopolitics*, 17/3, 2012, pp. 502–25.

2 ORDERING TIME

1. Jean-Claude Juncker cited in 'European MPs vote to end summer time clock changes', *BBC News*, 26 March 2019. The new regulation has been backed by the European Parliament, but it has not been adopted by the Council so far. See Arthur Beesley, 'Clock stops on EU plan to scrap daylight savings time', *Irish Times*, 26 March 2021.

2. Christopher McIntosh, 'The Trump Administration's Politics of Time: The Temporal Dynamics that Enable Trump's Interests to Determine American Foreign Policy', *Time & Society*, 29/2, 2020, pp. 362–91.

3. Jenny Shaw, '"Winning Territory": Changing Place to Change Pace', in *Timespace: Geographies of Temporalities*, John May and Nigel Thrift, eds, Routledge, London, 2001, pp. 120–32.

4. Carlo Rovelli, *The Order of Time*, Penguin, London, 2018, p. 17.

5. Gevin Giorbran, 'Albert Einstein and the Fabric of Time', in *Everything Forever: Learning to See Timelessness*, http://everythingforever.com/einstein.htm.

6. Rovelli, *Order of Time*, p. 21.

7. Julian Barbour, 'The Nature of Time', 1 December 2008, http://www.platonia.com/nature_of_time_ essay.pdf.

8. Julian Barbour, *The End of Time: The Next Revolution in Physics*, Oxford University Press, Oxford, New York, 1999, p. 251.

9. Rovelli, *Order of Time*, pp. 3 and 202.

10. Lee Smolin, *Time Reborn: From the Crisis in Physics to the Future of the Universe*, Houghton Mifflin Harcourt, Boston, MA, 2013, p. xii.

11. Ibid., p. xiv.

12. Helga Nowotny, *Time: The Modern and Post-Modern Experience*, Polity Press, Cambridge, 1994, p. 143.

13. Norbert Elias, *Time: An Essay*, Blackwell, London, 1992, p. 12.

14. Barbara Adam, *Time*, Polity Press, Cambridge, 2004, p. 122.

15. Thomas M. Allen, *A Republic in Time: Temporality and Social Imagination in Nineteenth-Century America*, University of North Carolina Press, Chapel Hill, NC, 2008, p. 2. Of course, historical transitions do not happen overnight. As Allen points out, initially clock time was understood as significantly different from natural and religious time, but it was also deeply intertwined with those other temporal modes.

16. Robert Hassan, 'Network Time and the New Knowledge Epoch', *Time and Society*, 12, 2003, p. 235.

17. Stephen Bertman, *Hyperculture: The Human Cost of Speed*, Praeger, London, 1998.

18. Time open to or shared by all can also be called public time. In the literature we also come across a distinction between 'private time' referring to 'subjective' temporal experiences and 'public time' referring to 'objective' measures of time. See for example Stephen E. Hanson, 'Objective and Subjective Time in Comparative Politics', in *The Oxford Handbook of Time and Politics*, Klaus H. Goetz, ed., https://doi.org/10.1093/oxfordhb/9780190862084.013. Also Eviatar Zerubavel, 'Private Time and Public Time: The Temporal Structure of Social Accessibility and Professional Commitments', *Social Forces*, 58/1, 1979, pp. 38–58.

19. Charles S. Maier, 'The Politics of Time: Changing Paradigms of Collective Time and Private Time in the Modern Era', in *Changing Boundaries of the Political: Essays on the Evolving Balance between the State and Society, Public and Private in Europe*, Charles S. Maier, ed., Cambridge University Press, New York, 1987, p. 155.

20. Maier, 'The Politics of Time', p. 154.

21. Ian Beacock, 'The Creation of (Modern) Time', *The Atlantic*, 22 December 2015, https://www.theatlantic.com/technology/archive/2015/12/the-creation-of-modern-time/421419/. See also Vanessa Ogle, *The Global Transformation of Time, 1870–1950*, Harvard University Press, Cambridge, MA, 2015.

22. Thomas M. Allen, *A Republic in Time: Temporality and Social Imagination in Nineteenth-Century America*, University of North Carolina Press, Chapel Hill, NC, 2008.

23. Allen, *A Republic in Time*, p. 7.

24. Ibid., p. 4.

25. Oliver Zimmer, 'One Clock Fits All? Time and Imagined Communities in Nineteenth-Century Germany', *Central European History*, 53/1, March 2020, pp. 48–70. See also Oliver Zimmer, *Remaking the Rhythms of Life: German Communities in the Age of the Nation-State*, Oxford University Press, Oxford, 2019.

26. Helmuth von Moltke, 'Gesammelte Schriften und Denkwürdigkeiten', in *Reden des Generalfeldmarschalls Helmuth von Moltke*, Bd 7, Mittler, Berlin, 1892, pp. 38–9.

27. Zimmer, 'One Clock Fits All?', p. 58.

28. Mehmet Kendirci, 'Time as an Instrument of Building Citizenship in Turkey in the Late Ottoman and the Early Republican Era', *Études balkaniques*, 2, 2017, p. 341.

29. Alexis McCrossen, *Marking Modern Times: A History of Clocks, Watches, and Other Timekeepers in American Life*, University of Chicago Press, Chicago, IL, 2013. Also David Rooney, *About Time: A History of Civilization in Twelve Clocks*, Norton, New York, 2021.
30. Randall Stevenson, *Reading the Times: Temporality and History in Twentieth-Century Fiction*, Edinburgh University Press, Edinburgh, 2018.
31. Zimmer, 'One Clock Fits All?', p. 48.
32. Randall Stevenson, *Reading the Times*, illustrates this point very well.
33. Émile Durkheim, *Les formes élémentaires de la vie religieuse*, F. Alcan, Paris, 1912, p. 7. Also Zerubavel, 'Private Time and Public Time', p. 40.
34. Stephen Kern, *The Culture of Time and Space, 1880–1918*, Harvard University Press, Cambridge, MA, 1983.
35. Maier, 'The Politics of Time', p. 159.
36. Stephen E. Hanson, *Time and Revolution: Marxism and the Design of Soviet Institutions*, University of North Carolina Press, Chapel Hill, NC, 1997, p. viii.
37. It should be noted that some historians, such as Christopher Clark, believe that the conception of time articulated by Nazi Germany was different from that articulated by other totalitarian regimes, not just the Soviet, but also the Italian Fascist regime. See Christopher Clark, *Time and Power: Visions of History in German Politics, from the Thirty Years' War to the Third Reich*, Princeton University Press, Princeton, NJ, 2019, p. 3.
38. Elizabeth F. Cohen, *The Political Value of Time: Citizenship, Duration, and Democratic Justice*, Cambridge University Press, Cambridge, 2018, p. 4.
39. Ibid.
40. Clark, *Time and Power*, p. 1.
41. David S. Landes, *Revolution in Time: Clocks and the Making of the Modern World*, Harvard University Press, Cambridge, MA, 1983, p. 33.
42. The notable exceptions include *The Oxford Handbook of Historical Institutionalism*, Orfeo Fioretos, Tulia G. Falleti and Adam Sheingate, eds, Oxford University Press, Oxford, 2016; *The Oxford Handbook of Time and Politics*, Klaus H. Goetz, ed., already cited in Chapter 1. See also Paul Pierson, *Politics in Time: History, Institutions and Social Analysis*, Princeton University Press, Princeton, NJ, 2004.
43. Ryszard Kapuściński, *Heban*, Czytelnik, Warsaw, 1998, p. 3. (My translation. The English edition of this book was published in 2002 by Penguin under the title *The Shadow of the Sun: My African Life*.)

3 NOMADS AND SETTLERS

1. The categories of nomads and settlers are not set in stone. The European colonizers of America or Australia started as nomads embracing 'open space', but in time turned into settlers building fences and walls. See for example Alan Taylor, *Colonial America: A Very Short Introduction*, Oxford University Press, Oxford, 2012. Also John G. Turner, *They Knew They Were Pilgrims: The Plymouth Colony and the Contest for American Liberty*, Yale University Press, New Haven, CT, 2020.

2. In many languages, terms such as space, territory or place are synonyms, but scholars have attributed different meanings to these terms. For details, see for example Fabio Duarte, *Space, Place and Territory: A Critical Review on Spatialities*, Routledge, London, 2018. Assigning a simple meaning to borders is also tricky. As Étienne Balibar argued: 'The idea of a simple definition of what constitutes a border is, by definition, absurd: to mark out a border is, precisely, to define a territory, to delimit it, and so to register the identity of that territory, or confer one upon it. Conversely, however, to define or identify in general is nothing other than to trace a border, to assign boundaries or borders (in Greek, hams; in Latin, finis or terminus; in German, Grenze; in French, borne). The theorist who attempts to define what a border is, is in danger of going round in circles, as the very representation of the border is the precondition for any definition.' See Étienne Balibar, *Politics and the Other Scene*, Verso, London, 2002, pp. 75–6.

3. Saskia Sassen, *Expulsions: Brutality and Complexity in the Global Economy*, Harvard University Press, Cambridge, MA, 2014, pp. 1–11.

4. Mathew Longo, *The Politics of Borders: Sovereignty, Security, and the Citizen after 9/11*, Cambridge University Press, Cambridge, 2018, p. xv.

5. James W. Scott, 'Introduction to a Research Agenda for Border Studies', in *A Research Agenda for Border Studies*, James W. Scott, ed., Edward Elgar Publishing, Cheltenham, 2020, p. 6.

6. Stanley Kubrick and Arthur C. Clarke, *2001: A Space Odyssey*, screenplay available at precede by www. or https://? archiviokubrick.it.

7. Stephen D. Krasner, *Sovereignty: An Organized Hypocrisy*, Princeton University Press, Princeton, NJ, 1999.

8. A. John Simmons, *Boundaries of Authority*, Oxford University Press, Oxford, 2016, p. 213.

9. Scott, 'Introduction to a Research Agenda for Border Studies', p. 3.

10. John Gerard Ruggie, 'Continuity and Transformation in the World Polity: Towards a Neorealist Synthesis', *World Politics*, 35, 1983, p. 274, quoting J.R. Strayer and D.C. Munro, *The Middle Ages 395–1500*, Appleton Century, New York, 1942, and Perry Anderson, *Lineages of the Absolutist State*, New Left Books, London, 1974.

11. Alexander C. Diener and Joshua Hagen, *Borders: A Very Short Introduction*, Oxford University Press, Oxford, 2012, pp. 1 and 4.

12. Henk van Houtum and Ton van Naerssen, 'Bordering, Ordering and Othering', *Tijdschrift voor economische en sociale geografie*, 93/2, 2002, pp. 125–36.

13. Francesca Mannocchi, 'Torture, rape and murder: Inside Tripoli's refugee detention camps', *Guardian*, 3 November 2019.

14. 'The Calais Jungle . . . three years on', helprefugees.org. The latest statistics regarding refugees can be found at the UNHCR website: https://www.unhcr.org/refugee-statistics/.

15. Paul Scheffer, *Freedom of the Border*, Polity Press, Cambridge, 2021, p. 10.

16. See for example Dan Rabinowitz, 'National Identity on the Frontier: Palestinians in the Israeli Education System', in *Border Identities: Nation and State at International Frontiers*, Thomas M. Wilson and Hastings Donnan, eds, Cambridge University Press, Cambridge, 1998, pp. 142–61.

17. Olga Tokarczuk, *Bieguni*, Wydawnictwo Literackie, Warsaw, 2019, p. 65. The motivation of the Nobel Prize Committee: 'For a narrative imagination that with encyclopaedic passion represents the crossing of boundaries as a form of life', www.nobelprize.org/prizes/literature/2018/tokarczuk/facts/.

18. Peter Sloterdijk, 'Talking to myself about the poetics of space', *Harvard Design Magazine*, 30, 2009.

19. Aleksandr Solzhenitsyn, *The Gulag Archipelago*, abridged, 50th-anniversary edition, Vintage, London, 2018, p. 544. See also Anne Applebaum, *Gulag: A History*, Doubleday, New York, 2003.

20. Kenneth Pomeranz, 'Empire & "Civilizing" Missions, Past & Present', *Dædalus*, 134, 2005, pp. 34–45.

21. Tokarczuk, *Bieguni*, p. 8.

22. UNHCR, https://www.unhcr.org/refugee-statistics/.

23. 'More Bulgarians working abroad than in Bulgaria', Sofia News Agency, 6 November 2015, novinite.com.

24. See wearenomads.com.

25. Michele Capecchi, 'Digital nomads in Italy: Visas and tax incentives for remote workers', *The Florentine*, 13 April 2021, theflorentine.net.

26. David Goodhart, *The Road to Somewhere: The Populist Revolt and the Future of Politics*, Hurst, London, 2017, p. 5.

27. Goodhart, *Road to Somewhere*.

28. Maier, *Once within Borders*, p. 290. See also the World Bank report, 'Bankers without Borders', World Bank Group, Washington, DC, 2018.

29. Ruud Koopmans and Michael Zürn, 'Cosmopolitanism and Communitarianism – How Globalization Is Reshaping Politics in the Twenty-First Century', in *The Struggle over Borders: Cosmopolitanism and Communitarianism*, Pieter de Wilde, Ruud Koopmans, Wolfgang Merkel, Oliver Strijbis and Michael Zürn, eds, Cambridge University Press, Cambridge, 2019, p. 3.

30. John Allen, 'Power's Quiet Reach and Why It Should Exercise Us', *Space and Polity*, 24/3, 2020, pp. 408–13.

31. Peter Sloterdijk, *Bubbles: Spheres I*, Wieland Hoban, trans., Semiotext(e), Los Angeles, CA, 2011, p. 478. Also Eli Pariser, 'Beware online "filter bubbles"', TED Talk, 2011, www.ted.com/talks/eli_pariser_beware_online_filter_bubbles.

32. James H. Dickinson, Commander's Strategic Vision, Commander's Foreword, United States Space Command, spacecom.mil, 2021.

33. Stewart M. Patrick, 'Colonizing space won't solve our problems on Earth', 26 July 2021, www.worldpoliticsreview.com. Also Richard Seymour, 'Why the billionaire space race is the colonial fantasy reborn', *New Statesman*, 20 July 2021, or Daniel Deudney, *Space Expansionism: Planetary Geopolitics, and the Ends of Humanity*, Oxford University Press, Oxford, 2020.

34. A.C. Boley and M. Byers, 'Satellite mega-constellations create risks in Low Earth Orbit, the atmosphere and on Earth', *Sci-Rep* 11/10642, 2021, https://doi.org/10.1038/s41598-021-89909-7.

35. Cited in *Gazeta Wyborcza*: https://wyborcza.pl/7,75399,27288160,nowa-strategia-bezpieczenstwa-narodowego-rosji-putin-przedstawil.html. The official Russian text of the Strategy can be found at: Указ Президента Российской Федерации от 02.07.2021 № 400. Официальное опубликование правовых

актов · Официальный интернет-портал правовой информации (pravo. gov.ru.

36. Jürgen Hecker, 'Global tax deal backed by 130 nations', *TechXplore*, techxplore.com, 2021.

37. The 2018 Windrush scandal concerned British 'subjects' born chiefly in Caribbean countries who were wrongly detained, denied legal rights and deported or threatened with deportation from the United Kingdom by the Home Office. See Wendy Williams, 'Windrush lessons learned review', 2018, publishing.service.gov.uk.

38. Louise Amoore, 'Biometric Borders: Governing Mobilities in the War on Terror', *Political Geography*, 25/3, 2006, pp. 336–51.

39. Sandro Mezzadra and Brett Neilson, 'Between Inclusion and Exclusion: On the Topology of Global Space and Borders', *Theory, Culture and Society*, 29/4/5, 2012, pp. 58–75.

40. Anthony Giddens, *Modernity and Self-Identity: Self and Society in the Late Modern Age*, Stanford University Press, Stanford, CA, 1991; or Ronald Inglehart et al., *Changing Human Beliefs and Values, 1981–2007: A Cross-Cultural Sourcebook Based on the World Values Surveys and European Values Studies*, Siglo XXI, Mexico City, 2010.

41. Rogers Brubaker, 'The Dolezal Affair: Race, Gender, and the Micropolitics of Identity', *Ethnic and Racial Studies*, 39/3, 2016, p. 414. Also Rogers Brubaker, *Trans: Gender and Race in an Age of Unsettled Identities*, Princeton University Press, Princeton, NJ, 2017.

42. Olivier Roy, *Secularism Confronts Islam*, George Holoch, trans., Columbia University Press, New York, 2007.

43. Ben Quinn, 'Petition urges Cardiff University to cancel Germaine Greer lecture', *Guardian*, 23 October 2015.

44. WATCH: President Obama warns of danger of safe spaces at Howard grad speech, HuffPost, 12 May 2016.

45. Jacob L. Nelson and James G. Webster, 'The Myth of Partisan Selective Exposure: A Portrait of the Online Political News Audience', *Social Media+Society*, 3/3, 2017, pp. 1–13. Also Pablo Barberá, John T. Jost, Jonathan Nagler, Joshue J. Tucker and Richard Bonneau, 'Tweeting from Left to Right: Is Online Political Communication More Than an Echo Chamber?', *Psychological Science*, 26/10, 2015, pp. 1531–42.

46. Olga Onuch, Emma Matteo and Julian G. Waller, 'Mobilization, Mass Perceptions, and (Dis)information: "New" and "Old" Media Consumption Patterns and Protest', *Social Media + Society*, 7/2, 2021, pp. 1–18.

47. Plato, *Republic*, C.D.C. Reeve, ed., Hackett Publishing, New York, 1992, p. 186.

48. Sloterdijk, *Bubbles*, pp. 61, 67.

49. Eytan Bakshy, Solomon Messing and Lada A. Adamic, 'Exposure to Ideologically Diverse News and Opinion on Facebook', *Science*, 348/6239, 2015, pp. 1130–2.

50. Ernest Gellner, *Encounters with Nationalism*, Blackwell, Oxford, 1994, p. 65.

51. Kenan Malik, 'I love the football team but can't get tribal about England. What's going on?', *Guardian*, 4 July 2021.

52. Controversy surrounding the 2021 judgment of the US Court of Appeals for the 8th Circuit regarding the University of Iowa discrimination policy shows the scale of complexity here. See George F. Will, 'Academia's hostility to intellectual diversity suffers a courtroom setback', *Washington Post*, 28 July 2021.

53. Paulina Ochoa Espejo, *On Borders: Territories, Legitimacy and the Rights of Place*, Oxford University Press, Oxford, 2020, pp. 13–20.

4 HIGH-SPEED REGIMES

1. *High-Speed Society: Social Acceleration, Power and Modernity*, Hartmut Rosa and William E. Scheuerman, eds, Penn State University Press, University Park, PA, 2009.

2. Behavioural scientists have shown that fast, instinctive and emotional thinking leads to irrational decisions in politics and economics. See Daniel Kahneman, *Thinking, Fast and Slow*, Farrar, Straus and Giroux, New York, 2011.

3. See Kwik Learning, https://kwiklearning.com/#:~:text=Kwik%20Learning%20is%20a%20powerhouse,and%20activate%20your%20inner%20genius.

4. Hartmut Rosa, 'Social Acceleration: Ethical and Political Consequences of a Desynchronized High-Speed Society', *Constellations*, 10/1, 2003, pp. 6–9. For an open-ended approach to acceleration see James Gleick, *Faster: The Acceleration of Just About Everything*, Pantheon, New York, 1999.

5. Paul Virilio, *L'horizon négatif*, Galilée, Paris, 1984, p. 59; Carmen Leccardi, 'Resisting "Acceleration Society"', *Constellations*, 10/1, 2003, pp. 39–40; Jeremy Rifkin, *Time Wars: The Primary Conflict in Human History*, H. Holt & Co., New York, 1987.

6. Manuel Castells, *The Rise of the Network Society, Vol 1: The Information Age: Economy, Society and Culture*, Blackwell, Oxford, 1996, pp. 470–71.

7. Ben Agger, 'Time Robbers, Time Rebels', in *24/7: Time and Temporality in the Network Society*, Robert Hassan and Ronald E. Purser, eds, Stanford University Press, Stanford, CA, 2007, p. 225. See also Ben Agger, *Speeding Up Fast Capitalism: Cultures, Jobs, Families, Schools, Bodies*, Routledge, London, 2004, especially pp. 1–32.

8. See Lucy Abbersteen, 'Line of Duty acronyms decoded: All the abbreviations explained', *Woman & Home*, 28 April 2021, womanandhome.com; or Michael Hogan, 'Line of Duty acronyms: Your essential guide to all the police terms and jargon, including CHIS and OCG', *Daily Telegraph*, 2 May 2021. Were I still interested in medieval manuscripts I would use digital tools to read all the abbreviations because in the 1970s it took me and my experienced professor up to a month to translate into Latin a few sentences. For those interested in reading medieval handwriting I recommend Yvonne Seale, 'A BEGINNER'S GUIDE TO DIGITAL PALAEOGRAPHY OF MEDIEVAL MANUSCRIPTS', 26 March 2016, https://yvonneseale.org/blog/2016/03/26/dh-palaeography/.

9. See www.urbandictionary.com. The motto adopted by the dictionary is: Define Your World.

10. This term was coined by Castells, *Rise of the Network Society*, p. 469.

11. John Naughton, 'Working from home was the dream but is it turning into a nightmare?', *Guardian*, 15 August 2020.

12. Jonathan Crary, *24/7: Late Capitalism and the Ends of Sleep*, Verso, London, 2013, pp. 9–10.

13. Kalyeena Makortoff, 'PwC's UK staff to split office and homeworking after Covid crisis', *Guardian*, 31 March 2021.

14. Ibid.

15. Meredith Turits, 'Could a "workcation" change how you think?', *BBC Worklife*, 20 March 2020.

16. See Workcations Blogs, www.workcactions.in/blog.

17. Beata Javorcik, Chief Economist for the European Bank for Reconstruction and Development, has illustrated how lockdowns have entrenched gender roles and set back equality. See 'How the glass ceiling survived the pandemic', *Politico*, 28 May 2021.

18. 'The Rise of Working from Home. Special Report', *The Economist*, 10 April 2021.

19. E.P. Thomson, 'Time, Work-Discipline, and Industrial Capitalism', *Past and Present*, 36, 1967, pp. 57–97.

20. Bob Jessop, 'The Spatiotemporal Dynamics of Globalizing Capital and their Impact on State Power and Democracy', in *High-Speed Society*, Rosa and Scheuerman, eds, pp. 135–58.

21. Elena Sánchez Nicolás, 'MEPs call for workers to have "right to disconnect"', euobserver.com, 25 January 2021. See also 'Citigroup CEO ordains Zoom-free Fridays to ease "relentless" pandemic workday', msn.com, 2021.

22. Régis Debray, 'Time Is to Politics What Space Is to Geometry', 'Time and Politics', in *Prison Writings*, Random House, New York, 1973, p. 90.

23. Robert Hassan, *Empires of Speed: Time and the Acceleration of Politics and Society*, Brill, Leiden, 2009, p. 6.

24. Giovanni Sartori, 'Video-Power', *Government and Opposition*, 24/1, 1989, p. 39.

25. Agamben, *State of Exception*. Also White, *Politics of Last Resort*.

26. William Scheuerman, *Liberal Democracy and the Social Acceleration of Time*, Johns Hopkins University Press, Baltimore, MA, 2004, p. 49.

27. See for example 'Poland declares state of emergency on Belarus border amid migrant surge', Reuters, 2 September 2021. Also Daniel Innerarity, 'Political Decision-Making in a Pandemic', in *Pandemics, Politics, and Society*, Gerard Delanty, ed., De Gruyter, Berlin, 2021, pp. 93–103.

28. Ming-Sung Kuo, 'Against Instantaneous Democracy', *I•CON*, 2019, p. 554.

29. Ibid., p. 570.

30. Paul Virilio, *Speed and Politics*, Mark Polizzotti, trans., Semiotext(e), New York, 1986, p. 142.

31. 'Tortoise, A Modern Fable', tortoisemedia.com. See also Maggie Berg and Barbara K. Seeber, *The Slow Professor: Challenging the Culture of Speed in the Academy*, University of Toronto Press, Toronto, 2016.

32. William E. Connolly, 'Speed, Concentric Cultures, and Cosmopolitanism', in *High-Speed Society*, Rosa and Scheuerman, eds, p. 263.

33. Ralf Dahrendorf, 'Has the East Joined the West?', *New Perspective Quarterly*, 7/2, Spring 1990, p. 42.

34. Judy Wajcman, *Pressed for Time: The Acceleration of Life in Digital Capitalism*, University of Chicago Press, Chicago, IL, 2015, p. 176.

35. Danny Dorling, *Slowdown: The End of the Great Acceleration – and Why It's Good for the Planet, the Economy, and our Lives*, Yale University Press, New Haven and London, 2020, p. 291.

36. Ibid., p. 294.

37. This is what sustainability economics does well. See Stefan Baumgärtner and Martin Quaas, 'What Is Sustainability Economics?', *Ecological Economics*, 69/13, 15 January 2010, pp. 445–50.

38. Robert and Edward Skidelsky, *How Much Is Enough? The Love of Money, and the Case for the Good Life*, Penguin, London, 2013. Also Tim Jackson, *Prosperity without Growth: Foundations for the Economy of Tomorrow*, Routledge, London, 2016.

39. Helga Nowotny, *In AI We Trust: Power, Illusion and Control of Predictive Algorithms*, Polity Press, Cambridge, 2021. Also Tom Chivers, *The AI Does Not Hate You: Superintelligence, Rationality and the Race to Save the World*, Weidenfeld & Nicolson, London, 2019.

40. Elinor Ostrom, *Governing the Commons: The Evolution of Institutions for Collective Action*, Cambridge University Press, Cambridge, 1990.

41. Chris Benner and Manuel Pastor, *Solidarity Economics: Why Mutuality and Movements Matter*, Polity Press, Cambridge, 2021.

42. The case for urgency was well articulated in Kevin P. Gallagher and Richard Kozul-Wright, *The Case for a New Bretton Woods*, Polity Press, Cambridge, 2022, pp. 10–21.

43. Rifkin, *Time Wars*.

44. *9 to 5*, film directed by Colin Higgins.

45. Robert E. Goodin, James Mahmud Rice, Antti Parpo and Lina Erikson, *Discretionary Time: A New Measure of Freedom*, Cambridge University Press, Cambridge, 2008, especially pp. 27–60. The authors argue that we need to replace money with time as the measure of freedom. We should query how much control citizens of OECD countries have over their allotments of time.

46. Hassan, *Empires of Speed*, p. 153.

5 MISMANAGED ROWDY SPACES

1. *Katyń*, film directed by Andrzej Wajda, 2007, available on YouTube, www.youtube.com/watch?v=V1RmYD3OOik.

2. Zygmunt Bauman with Ezio Mauro, *Babel*, Polity Press, Cambridge, 2016, p. 4.

3. The quotes and metaphor of lottery are borrowed from Bauman and Mauro, *Babel*, p. 1. The original quotes can be found in Jorge Luis Borges, *Collective Fictions*, Andrew Hurley, trans., Penguin, London, 1999, pp. 101–6.

4. Pierre Hassner, 'An Overview of the Problem', in *War and Peace: European Conflict Prevention, Chaillot Paper No. 11*, Nicole Gnessotto, ed., Institute for Security Studies, Western European Union, Paris, 1993, p. 7.

5. Richard Rosecrance, 'The Rise of the Virtual State', *Foreign Affairs*, 75/4, 1996, pp. 45–61. See also Thomas L. Friedman, *The World is Flat. A Brief History of the Twenty-first Century*, Farrar, Straus and Giroux, New York, 2005.

6. *Connectivity Wars: Why Migration, Finance and Trade are the Geo-Economic Battlegrounds of the Future*, Mark Leonard, ed., ECFR, London, 2016. Also *The Uses and Abuses of Weaponized Interdependence*, Daniel W. Drezner, Henry Farrell and Abraham L. Newman, eds, Brookings Institution Press, Washington, DC, 2021.

7. Jeffrey Rothfeder, 'The great unravelling of globalization', *Washington Post*, 24 April 2015.

8. The technological sophistication of modern weapons made 'people's armies', relying chiefly on conscripts, obsolete. See Conrad C. Crane, *Transforming Defense*, Strategic Studies Institute, US Army War College, Carlisle Barracks, PA, 2001.

9. For some background analysis see for example Rory Archer, 'Assessing Turbofolk Controversies: Popular Music between the Nation and the Balkans', *Southeastern Europe*, 36, 2012, pp. 178–207.

10. Azeem Ibrahim, 'Reducing America's dependence on China is now a strategic necessity', *National Interest*, 16 April 2020.

11. Duffy Toft, *Geography of Ethnic Violence*, p. 1.

12. However, it should be stressed that, statistically, the link between religious and violent radicalization is very weak and few terrorists belong to fundamentalist religious communities. See Olivier Roy, 'Religion and the state: Unintended effects of anti-radicalisation policies', *OpenDemocracy*, 19 July 2021.

13. For a recent discussion on the obsolescence of war see Michael Mousseau, 'The End of War: How a Robust Marketplace and Liberal Hegemony Are Leading to Perpetual World Peace', *International Security*, 44/1, 2019, pp. 160–96; Tanisha M. Fazal and Paul Poast, 'War Is Not Over', *Foreign Affairs*, 98/6, 2019, pp. 73–83.

14. Of course, other factors were also at play here. The wall would not have fallen without a vibrant civil society demanding reforms in Poland, and in other countries of the region. See Jacques Rupnik, *The Other Europe: The Rise and Fall of Communism in East-Central Europe*, Weidenfeld & Nicolson, London, 1988; and Grzegorz Ekiert and Jan Kubik, *Rebellious Civil Society: Popular Protest and Democratic Consolidation in Poland, 1989–1993*, University of Michigan Press, Ann Arbor, MI, 1999. Other experts point to President Reagan's 'Star Wars' project as a contributing factor. See for example Philip D. Zelikow and Condoleezza Rice, *Germany Unified and Europe Transformed: A Study in Statecraft*, Harvard University Press, Cambridge, MA, 1997; and Gale Stokes, *The Walls Came Tumbling Down: The Collapse of Communism in Eastern Europe*, Oxford University Press, Oxford, 1993, p. 71.

15. 'Robin Cook's speech on the government's ethical foreign policy', *Guardian*, 12 May 1997.

16. See for example Grzegorz W. Kolodko, *China and the Future of Globalization: The Political Economy of China's Rise*, Bloomsbury Publishing, London, 2020.

17. See for example Joris Luyendijk, *Swimming with Sharks: My Journey into the World of Bankers*, Faber & Faber, London, 2015. Also Naomi Klein, *Fences and Windows: Dispatches from the Front Lines of the Globalization Debate*, Flamingo, New York, 2002.
18. Joseph Stiglitz, *Making Globalization Work*, Penguin, London, 2006, p. xii.
19. Ibid., p. ix.
20. China was granted 'most favoured nation' status in 1979. Mike Collins cites Robert Scott's estimates in 'The pros and cons of globalization', *Forbes*, 6 May 2015.
21. Laurence Chandy and Brina Seidel, 'Donald Trump and the future of globalization', *Brookings*, 18 November 2016.
22. Jonah Birch and George Souvlis, interview with Wolfgang Streeck, 'Social democracy's last rounds', *Jacobin*, 25 February 2016.
23. Philip Bobbitt, *The Shield of Achilles: War, Peace, and the Course of History*, Alfred A. Knopf, New York, 2002, pp. xxi–xxxii.
24. Ibid., pp. 234–5.
25. See for example Tod Lindberg, 'The Return of the State', Hudson Institute, 15 April 2020. For an earlier and more elaborate version of this argument see especially *Bringing the State Back In*, Peter B. Evans, Dietrich Rueschemeyer and Theda Skocpol, eds, Cambridge University Press, Cambridge, 1985.
26. Fiona Harvey and Phoebe Cooke, 'UK ministers "met fossil fuel firms nine times as often as clean energy ones" ', *Guardian*, 10 September 2021.
27. Bauman and Mauro, *Babel*.
28. Klein, *Shock Doctrine*, pp. 289–99; Michael J. Sandel, *What Money Can't Buy: The Moral Limits of Markets*, Farrar, Straus and Giroux, New York, 2012.
29. Helen Thompson, 'The world to come: Revenge of the nation state', *New Statesman*, 26 August 2020.
30. Jan Zielonka, 'The EU as International Actor: Unique or Ordinary?', *European Foreign Affairs Review*, 16/3, 2011, pp. 281–301.
31. UNHCR, 'Syria refugee crisis explained', 8 July 2022, unrefugees.org. The Taliban takeover after the US withdrawal from Afghanistan in 2021 is likely to generate another flow of refugees. See 'Afghanistan: How many refugees are there and where will they go?', *BBC News*, 31 August 2021.
32. Philippe Droz-Vincent, 'The Renewed "Struggle for Syria": From the War "in" Syria to the War "over" Syria', *International Spectator*, 55/3, 2020, pp. 115–31.
33. Western states cultivated good if not friendly relations with Colonel Gaddafi of Libya, then intervened with military forces to depose him, leaving the country in the hands of the local warlords; they are now bribing these warlords to keep migrants off Libyan shores, with poor results, not surprisingly. See for example Libya, Migrant Report 37 (May–June 2021), *Flow Monitoring*, International Organization for Migration.
34. Christian Joppke, *Is Multiculturalism Dead? Crisis and Persistence in the Constitutional State*, Polity Press, Cambridge, 2017, pp. 2–3.
35. According to a study prepared by the World Bank, 200 million migrants spread throughout the world send home over US $300 billion per year, which dwarfs the amount of development aid and many other financial flows. See World Bank

document. See also F. Niyonkuru, 'Failure of Foreign Aid in Developing Countries: A Quest for Alternatives', *Business and Economics Journal*, 25 June 2016. Also Sebastian Edwards, 'Economic Development and the Effectiveness of Foreign Aid: A Historical Perspective', *Kyklos*, 68/3, 2015, pp. 277–316; Mark McGillivray, Simon Feeny, Niels Hermes and Robert Lensink, 'Controversies over the Impact of Development Aid: It Works; It Doesn't; It Can, but That Depends', *Journal of International Development*, 18/7, 2006, pp. 1031–50.

36. European Union member states that utilized a seven-year transition period for preparing social services ahead of the new labour influx have experienced much less political anxiety about working Poles and other Eastern Europeans than was the case in Great Britain. Bela Galgoczi, Janine Leschke and Andrew Watt, *EU Labour Migration in Troubled Times: Skills Mismatch, Return and Policy Responses*, Routledge, London, 2012.

37. The rapid increase in EU workers – 700,000 extra in 2012–15 – coincided with the increase of 1 million British people at work. See data provided by Charlie Cooper, 'EU referendum: immigration and Brexit – what lies have been spread?', *Independent*, 20 June 2016.

38. Linsey Smith, 'Brexit: Views from Boston, Britain's most eurosceptic town', *BBC News*, 23 June 2021.

39. See for example 'Is migration good for the economy?', *OECD Migration Policy Debates*, May 2014. Also OECD/ILO, 'How immigrants contribute to developing countries' economies', OECD Publishing, Paris, 2018.

40. Nick Vaughan-Williams, *Vernacular Border Security: Citizens' Narratives of Europe's 'Migration Crisis'*, Oxford University Press, Oxford, 2021, pp. 4–7.

41. Anne-Marie Slaughter, 'Anne-Marie Slaughter on why America's diversity is its strength', *The Economist*, 24 August 2021. For a critical analysis see Roxanne Dunbar-Ortiz, *Not 'A Nation of Immigrants': Settler Colonialism, White Supremacy, and a History of Erasure and Exclusion*, Beacon Press, Boston, MA, 2021.

42. See especially Andrew Geddes, *Governing Migration beyond the State: Europe, North America, and Southeast Asia in a Global Context*, Oxford University Press, Oxford, 2021. Also Alexander Betts and Paul Collier, *Refugee: Transforming a Broken Refugee System*, Allen Lane, London, 2017.

43. Hein de Haas, 'International Migration, Remittances and Development: Myths and Facts', *Third World Quarterly*, 26/8, 2015, pp. 1269–84. Also Douglas S. Massey, Jorge Durand and Nolan J. Malone, *Beyond Smoke and Mirrors: Mexican Immigration in an Era of Economic Integration*, Russell Sage Foundation, New York, 2002.

44. Patrick Wintour, 'Afghanistan's neighbours offered millions in aid to harbour refugees', *Guardian*, 31 August 2021.

45. Radina Gigova, Sharon Braithwaite, Jorge Engels, Sarah Diab and Bethlehem Feleke, 'UK-Rwanda migrant deal: UK announces controversial plan to send asylum-seekers to Rwanda', CNN, 15 April 2022.

46. 'Climate change 2021: The physical science basis', IPCC, 9 August 2021.

47. See for example Mark Maslin, *How to Save our Planet*, Penguin, London, 2021; Danny Cullenward and David G. Victor, *Making Climate Policy Work*, Polity Press, Cambridge, 2020; Chris Forman and Claire Asher, *Brave New World: How Science Can Save Our Planet*, Unipress, Cambridge, MA, 2021.

48. 'BP sets ambition for net zero by 2050, fundamentally changing organisation to deliver', BP website, News and Insights, www.bp.com/en/global/corporate/news-and-insights/press-releases/bernard-looney-announces-new-ambition-for-bp.html; Leon, 'The Future of Fast Food is Better for the planet', https://leon.co/presents/read/the-future-of-fast-food-is-better-for-the-planet/.

49. Quirin Schiermeier, 'Eat less meat: UN climate-change report calls for change to human diet', Nature, 8 August 2019, www.nature.com/articles/d41586-019-02409-7; 'Environmental benefits of public transportation', Greentumble, 2 October 2016.

50. Tess Riley, 'Just 100 companies responsible for 71% of global emissions, study says', Guardian, 10 July 2017.

51. Paul G. Harris, *Pathologies of Climate Governance*, Cambridge University Press, Cambridge, 2021, p. 5.

52. Oliver Milman, 'James Hansen, father of climate change awareness, calls Paris talks "a fraud"', Guardian, 12 December 2015.

53. Ibid. It should be noted, however, that the Paris Agreement has become a focal point of climate change litigation. For instance, in May 2021, the court ordered Royal Dutch Shell to reduce its global carbon emissions from its 2019 levels by 45% by 2030. See Daniel Boffey, 'Court orders Royal Dutch Shell to cut carbon emissions by 45% by 2030', Guardian, 26 May 2021.

54. Warren Cornwall, 'The Paris Climate Pact Is 5 Years Old. Is it Working?', Science, www.science.org/content/article/paris-climate-pact-5-years-old-it-working; Lindsay Maizland, 'Global climate agreements: Successes and failures,' Council on Foreign Relations, 17 November 2021.

55. 'Greta on Cop26, even more vague contents than bla bla bla', Limited Times, newsrnd.com.

56. 'End Climate Betrayal' sign held by activists in the UK, YouTube, https://www.youtube.com/watch?v=7bGYMfLifzM.

57. Joschka Fischer, 'National Egoism vs. Planetary Responsibility', Project Syndicate, 20 August 2021.

58. Julia Costa Lopez, 'political authority in international relations: revisiting the medieval debate', International Organization, Cambridge Core, Cambridge University Press, 14 January 2020; Julia Costa Lopez, '*Merum Imperium* and Sovereignty in the Later Middle Ages', International Studies Review, 20/3, 2018, pp. 489–519.

59. Jan-Werner Müller, 'Why culture wars are an elite device', New Statesman, 2 September 2021.

60. See for example Philippe Nonet and Philip Selznick, *Law and Society in Transition: Towards Responsive Law*, Routledge, London, 2016.

61. Robert A. Dahl, 'A Democratic Dilemma: System Effectiveness versus Citizen Participation', Political Science Quarterly, 109/1, 1994, p. 33.

62. Milan Kundera, *The Art of the Novel*, Faber & Faber, London, 2005, p. 115.

6 POLITICAL PAST AND FUTURE

1. Vladimir Putin, 'On the Historical Unity of Russians and Ukrainians', President of Russia, 12 July 2021.

2. Victoria Smolkin, 'Fantasy is not history', *Meduza*, 24 February 2022. For a comprehensive and nuanced analysis of the region's history see especially Timothy Snyder, *Bloodlands: Europe between Hitler and Stalin*, Basic Books, New York, 2010. Also Anne Applebaum, *Red Famine: Stalin's War on Ukraine, 1921–1933*, Doubleday, New York, 2017.

3. Billy Perrigo, 'How Putin's denial of Ukraine's statehood rewrites history', *Time*, 22 February 2022; 'Putin calls Ukrainian statehood a fiction: History suggests otherwise', *New York Times*, 21 February 2022.

4. Max Cohen, 'Trump blasts Birx after she warns coronavirus pandemic is "extraordinarily widespread"', *Politico*, 8 March 2020; Melissa Quinn and Margaret Brennan, 'Birx says there was no "full-time team" working on Covid response in Trump White House', *CBS News*, 25 January 2021.

5. According to an opinion poll carried out by YouGov in 2014, 59 per cent of respondents in the UK thought the British empire was something to be proud of: see Will Dahlgreen, 'The British Empire is "something to be proud of"', *YouGov*, 26 July 2014. However, by March 2020, this percentage had almost halved, and stood at 32 per cent: see Richard J. Evans, 'The history wars', *New Statesman*, 23 June 2020. Also Hannah Rose Woods, *Rule, Nostalgia: A Backwards History of Britain*, W.H. Allen, London, 2022.

6. Andrew Roth, 'Russian court orders closure of country's oldest human rights group', *Guardian*, 28 December 2021. For the quote of Vladimir Putin cited here, see Alec Luhn, 'Gulag grave hunter unearths uncomfortable truths in Russia', *Guardian*, 1 August 2017. See also David Marples, 'Lukashenka seeks to rewrite history books', *Belarus News and Analysis*, minsk.by, 20 June 2006.

7. Keane, 'Thoughts on Uncertainty', pp. 1–13.

8. 'Mess' is a relative term because, as Helga Nowotny has shown, messiness reveals the different patterns of order and disorder: *An Orderly Mess*, Central European University Press, Budapest, 2017.

9. Susi Dennison and Tara Varma, 'A certain idea of Europe: How the next French president can lead', *European Council on Foreign Relations*, 9 March 2022.

10. I found one of these monuments abandoned on the outskirts of the Dutch city of Groningen.

11. 'Leopold II statues defaced and removed across Belgium', *The Bulletin*, 15 June 2020.

12. '40% of GOP voters think civil war likely', *Rasmussen Reports*, 15 June 2020.

13. Ivan Krastev, 'We are all living in Vladimir Putin's world now', *New York Times*, 27 February 2022.

14. Katey Goodwin, 'Revealing the facts and figures of London's statues and monuments', *Art UK*, 21 October 2021.

15. The Commission for Diversity in the Public Realm, London City Hall, www.london.gov.uk/what-we-do/arts-and-culture/commission-diversity-public-realm.

16. Evans, 'The history wars'.

17. David W. Blight, 'The fog of history wars', *New Yorker*, 9 June 2021. For a study of who decides what history gets taught to American high-school

students, and how, see Gary B. Nash, Charlotte Antoinette Crabtree and Ross E. Dunn, *History on Trial: Culture Wars and the Teaching of the Past*, Vintage Books, New York, 2000.

18. Frances Yates, *The Art of Memory*, Chicago University Press, Chicago, IL, 1966, p. 20. Yates' concept of memory draws on the work of the Roman philosopher Cicero.

19. Richard Ned Lebow, 'The Memory of Politics in Postwar Europe', in *The Politics of Memory in Postwar Europe*, Richard Ned Lebow, Wulf Kansteiner and Claudio Fogu, eds, Duke University Press, London, 2006, pp. 8–16.

20. Xi Jinping cited in 'China's history wars: Controlling present, past and future', *Al Jazeera*, 1 July 2021.

21. Sergei Guriev and Daniel Treisman, *Spin Dictators: The Changing Face of Tyranny in the 21st Century*, Princeton University Press, Princeton, NJ, 2022.

22. See for example *History Wars: The Enola Gay and Other Battles for the American Past*, Edward T. Linethal and Tom Engelhardt, eds, H. Holt & Co., New York, 1996. Also *History Wars and the Classroom: Global Perspectives*, Tony Taylor and Robert Guyver, eds, Information Age Publishing, Charlotte, NC, 2012.

23. See for example *Contested Pasts: The Politics of Memory*, Katharine Hodgkin and Susannah Radstone, eds Routledge, London, 2003. Also *European Memory? Contested Histories and Politics of Remembrance*, Małgorzata Pakier and Bo Stråth, eds., Berghahn Books, Oxford, 2010.

24. Much depends on who writes the history, because historical interpretations tend to be biased. See for example Gayatri Chakravorty Spivak, 'Can the Subaltern Speak?', in *Marxism and the Interpretation of Culture*, Cary Nelson and Lawrence Grossberg, eds, Macmillan, London, 1988, pp. 271–313.

25. Milan Kundera, *The Book of Laughter and Forgetting*, Penguin, New York, 1990, p. 7.

26. John Keane, *The New Despotism*, Harvard University Press, Cambridge, MA, 2020, pp. 127–32.

27. Madeline Fry Schultz, '*Don't Look Up*: Another lazy anti-Trump movie', *Washington Examiner*, 30 December 2021. See also Peter Debruge, '*Don't Look Up* review: Adam McKay's apocalyptic comet comedy', *Variety*, 7 December 2021.

28. Branko Marcetic, 'Adam McKay's *Don't Look Up* captures the stupidity of our political era', *Jacobin*, 2 January 2022.

29. Peter Kalmus, 'I'm a climate scientist: *Don't Look Up* captures the madness I see every day', *Guardian*, 29 December 2021.

30. Ibid.

31. Ketan Joshi, Fiona Harvey, Nina Lakhani and Damian Carrington, '*Don't Look Up*: Four climate experts on the polarising disaster film', *Guardian*, 8 January 2022.

32. Christopher Wlezien, 'The Myopic Voter? The Economy and US Presidential Elections', *Electoral Studies*, 39, September 2015, pp. 195–204.

33. Adam Morton, 'Australian government seen globally as climate "denialist", UN summit observers say', *Guardian*, 24 September 2019.

34. Eurobarometer 90, November 2018.

35. Eri Bertsou, 'Political Distrust and its Discontents: Exploring the Meaning, Expression and Significance of Political Distrust', *Societies*, 9/72, 2019.

36. John Osborne, *Look Back in Anger*, Faber & Faber, London, 1956.

37. See Scheuerman, *Liberal Democracy*. Also *Global Democracy: Normative and Empirical Perspectives*, Daniele Archibugi, Mathias Koenig-Archibugi, Raffaele Marchetti, eds, Cambridge University Press, Cambridge, 2011. The topic of the global or transnational media should also be considered in this context. See W. Lance Bennett, 'Global Media and Politics: Transnational Communication Regimes and Civic Cultures', *Annual Review of Political Science*, 7/1, 2004, pp. 125–48; *Politics and the Media in New Democracies: Europe in a Comparative Perspective*, Jan Zielonka, ed., Oxford University Press, Oxford, 2015.

38. Graham Smith, *Can Democracy Safeguard the Future?*, Polity Press, Cambridge, 2021, p. 1.

39. The term 'colonizing the future' is used in Roman Krznaric, *The Good Ancestor: A Radical Prescription for Long-Term Thinking*, The Experiment, New York, 2020.

40. 'The Nuclear Priesthood', https://www.bbc.co.uk/programmes/p09vvw40.

41. William Hall, Anthony McDonnell and Jim O'Neill, *Superbugs: An Arms Race against Bacteria*, Harvard University Press, Cambridge, MA, 2018, p. 215.

42. David Runciman, *The Confidence Trap: A History of Democracy in Crisis from World War I to the Present*, Princeton University Press, Princeton, NJ, 2013.

43. See for example '*The Economist* crowns Draghi, Italy country of the year', ANSA.it, 16 December 2021. See also Christopher J. Bickerton and Carlo Invernizzi Accetti, *Technopopulism: The New Logic of Democratic Politics*, Oxford University Press, Oxford, 2021.

44. See *Institutions for Future Generations*, Iñigo González-Ricoy and Axel Gosseries, eds, Oxford University Press, Oxford, 2016. Also *Regulating Europe*, Giandomenico Majone, ed., Routledge, London, 1996.

45. Governments of EU member states delegate certain policies to the EU in order to bypass their national parliaments. The latter can formally block individual decisions taken in Brussels, but unpacking complex European deals is a drastic option undermining the entire integration project, hence the reluctance to use this option. See Chris J. Bickerton, *European Integration: From Nation-States to Member States*, Oxford University Press, Oxford, 2013.

46. See for example Jana Thompson, *Intergenerational Justice: Rights and Responsibilities in an Intergenerational Polity*, Routledge, London, 2009. Also Philippe van Parijs, 'The Disfranchisement of the Elderly, and Other Attempts to Secure Intergenerational Justice', *Philosophy & Public Affairs*, 27/4, 1998, pp. 292–333.

47. John Keane, 'The Age of Mega-Projects', January 2013, www.johnkeane.net/the-age-of-mega-projects.

48. Giorgio Locatelli, Giacomo Mariani, Tristano Sainati and Marco Greco, 'Corruption in Public Projects and Megaprojects: There is an Elephant in the Room!', *International Journal of Project Management*, 35/3, 2017, pp. 252–68.

49. Rajeev Syal, 'Abandoned NHS IT system has cost £10bn so far', *Guardian*, 18 September 2013; 'Spain's Ciudad Real airport sold at auction for €10,000', *BBC News*, 18 July 2015; Geoffrey Brumfiel, 'America's nuclear dumpsters: Why did Yucca Mountain fail, and what next?', *Slate*, 30 January 2013; 'Turow power plant expansion, Poland: Most efficient lignite-fired unit', nsenergy-business.com; and Kira Taylor, 'EU court orders immediate halt to Turów mine in Poland', Euractiv, 21 May 2021.

50. Pink Floyd, 'Time', video available at https://www.youtube.com/watch?v=AkawT3wjAb4

51. Angela Dewan, Aditi Sangal, Isabelle Jani-Friend, Melissa Mahtani and Meg Wagner, 'Climate protests led by youths spread across the world', CNN Live Updates, 24 September 2021.

52. See for example Donatella della Porta, *Mobilizing for Democracy: Comparing 1989 and 2011*, Oxford University Press, Oxford, 2014.

53. 'Third night of protests in Poland after abortion ban takes effect', *Guardian*, 29 January 2021; Tom Stevens, 'Poles protest over PiS "breaking constitution"', *Guardian*, 26 February 2016.

54. Quote by Donald Rumsfeld: 'There are known knowns, things we know that we . . .', Donald Rumsfeld, *Known and Unknown: A Memoir*, Sentinel, 2011. For the information gap in making long-term policies see for example Alan M. Jacobs, 'Policy Making for the Long Term in Advanced Democracies', *Annual Review of Political Science*, 19, 2016, pp. 433–54.

55. See Ben Agger, *Fast Capitalism*, University of Illinois Press, Chicago, IL, 1988.

56. Parliament of Finland, Committee for the Future, eduskunta.fi; Linda Gessner, Knesset Commission for Future Generations, 25 June 2017.

57. Hungarian Parliament's Deputy Commissioner for Fundamental Rights, the Ombudsman for Future Generations, Foundation for Democracy and Sustainable Development; Office of the Children's Commissioner, New Zealand, occ.org.nz.

58. European Commission, 'Prospective stratégique' europa.eu.

59. Welsh Government, 'Well-being of Future Generations (Wales) Act 2015'. Also UK Parliament, 'Wellbeing of Future Generations Bill 2021', House of Lords Library.

60. Jonathan Boston, *Governing for the Future: Designing Democratic Institutions for a Better Tomorrow*, Emerald Group Publishing, Bingley, 2016, p. 15.

61. Nowotny, *In AI We Trust*, p. 11.

62. Niall Ferguson, 'Why the end of America's empire won't be peaceful', *The Economist*, 20 August 2021; John G. Ikenberry, *Liberal Leviathan: The Origins, Crisis, and Transformation of the American World Order*, Princeton University Press, Princeton, NJ, 2011.

63. Smith, *Can Democracy Safeguard the Future?*, p. 111.

7 FROM STATES TO NETWORKS

1. Ivan Krastev, 'What Europeans think about the US-China Cold War', European Council on Foreign Relations, 22 September 2021.

2. Bill Gates on Corona Virus in 2015, TED talk, available on YouTube, www.youtube.com/watch?v=QdSyKEBiOnE.

3. By governance, we understand the formation and functioning of rules, institutions and practices through which actors maintain order and achieve collective goals. See for example James N. Rosenau, 'Change, Complexity, and Governance in a Globalizing Space', in *Debating Governance: Authority,*

Steering and Democracy, Jon Pierre, ed., Oxford University Press, Oxford, 2000, pp. 167–200.

4. See especially Manuel Castells, *The Internet Galaxy: Reflections on the Internet, Business, and Society*, Oxford University Press, Oxford, 2001.

5. Niall Ferguson, *The Square and the Tower: Networks and Power, from the Freemasons to Facebook*, Penguin, New York, 2018, p. 18.

6. Networks have earned a prominent place in various kinds of conspiracy theories. See for example Mike Wendling, 'QAnon: What is it and where did it come from?', *BBC News*, 6 January 2021.

7. Hastings Rashdall, *The Universities of Europe in the Middle Ages*, Cambridge University Press, Cambridge, 2010,

8. Castells, *The Internet Galaxy*, p. 2.

9. The situation gets even more complex when we examine multimodal networks using algorithms, for instance. See David Knoke, Mario Diani, James Hollway and Dimitris Christopoulos, *Multimodal Political Networks*, Cambridge University Press, Cambridge, 2021.

10. See for example Deborah Avant and Oliver Westerwinter, *The New Power Politics: Networks and Transnational Security Governance*, Oxford University Press, Oxford, 2016.

11. Miles Kahler, 'Networked Politics: Agency, Power, and Governance', in *Networked Politics: Agency, Power, and Governance*, Miles Kahler, ed., Cornell University Press, Ithaca, NY, pp. 3–7.

12. See for example Bruno Latour, 'Networks, Society and Spheres: Reflections on an Actor-Network Theorist', *International Journal of Communication*, 5, 2011, p. 799.

13. Paul McLean, *Culture in Networks*, Polity Press, Cambridge, 2017, pp. 15–33.

14. Stephen D. Krasner, *Sovereignty, Organized Hypocrisy*, Princeton University Press, Princeton, NJ, 1999.

15. Although academic studies on networks originated in the 1930s, the birth of the so-called 'new science of networks' took place less than three decades ago. See for example Duncan J. Watts, *Six Degrees: The Science of a Connected Age*, Norton, New York, 2004. Also Charles Kadushin, *Understanding Social Networks: Concepts, Theories, and Findings*, Oxford University Press, Oxford, 2012.

16. Wendy Hall, 'The Ever Evolving Web: The Power of Networks', *International Journal of Communication*, 5, 2011, p. 652.

17. Carmine Gallo, 'Steve Jobs' advice: "Dream Bigger"', *Forbes*, 14 December 2010.

18. See Nick Bostrom, *Superintelligence: Paths, Dangers, Strategies*, Oxford University Press, Oxford, 2014; Yuval Noah Harari, *Homo Deus: A Brief History of Tomorrow*, Vintage, London, 2017.

19. See Kenan Malik, 'Think only authoritarian regimes spy on their citizens?', *Guardian*, 22 December 2019; Steven Feldstein, 'Governments are using spyware on citizens: Can they be stopped?', Carnegie Endowment for International Peace, 21 July 2021: Shaun Walker, 'Polish senators draft law to regulate spyware after anti-Pegasus testimony', *Guardian*, 24 January 2022.

20. Rory Cellan-Jones, 'Stephen Hawking warns artificial intelligence could end mankind', *BBC News*, 2 December 2014.

21. Samuel Gibbs, 'Elon Musk: Artificial intelligence is our biggest existential threat', *Guardian*, 27 October 2014.
22. Bostrom, *Superintelligence*.
23. Franz Kafka, *The Trial*, Vintage, London, 2001 (first published 1925).
24. 'Karel Capek and the Robot (Complete History)', *History Computer*, 19 October 2019, https://history-computer.com/karel-capek-and-the-robot-complete-history.
25. Nowotny, *In AI We Trust*, p. 117.
26. Ibid., p. 17.
27. See for example Adrian Daub, *What Tech Calls Thinking*, Macmillan, London, 2020; Anna Wiener, *Uncanny Valley: A Memoir*, MCD Books, New York, 2020; Alex Kantrowitz, *Always Day One: How the Tech Titans Plan to Stay on Top Forever*, Penguin, London, 2020.
28. 'Trump to launch new social media platform TRUTH Social', *BBC News*, 21 October 2021.
29. See Jaime E. Settle, *Frenemies: How Social Media Polarizes America*, Cambridge University Press, Cambridge, 2018; Sarah Frier, *No Filter: The Inside Story of Instagram*, Simon & Schuster, 2020.
30. Grace Graupe-Pillard, 'Facebook, YouTube censored my art: My only "sin" was revealing my elderly body', *True Jersey*, New Jersey, 9 November 2020.
31. Peter Dauvergne and Genevieve LeBaron, *Protest Inc.: The Corporatization of Activism*, Polity Press, Cambridge, 2014.
32. See Anna C. Vakil, 'Confronting the Classification Problem: Toward a Taxonomy of NGOs', *World Development*, 25/12, 1997, pp. 2057–70. Also *International Encyclopedia of Civil Society*, Helmut K. Anheier and Stefan Toepler, eds, Springer, New York, 2009, especially the section on Quangos by Lawrence S. Cumming.
33. See *Climate Urbanism: Towards a Critical Research Agenda*, Vanesa Castán Broto, Enora Robin and Aidan While, eds, Palgrave Macmillan, Cham, 2020; Raffaele Marchetti, *City Diplomacy: From City-States to Global Cities*, University of Michigan Press, Ann Arbor, MI, 2021; Saskia Sassen, *The Global City*, Princeton University Press, Princeton, NJ, 2013.
34. See for example *Urban Europe: Fifty Tales of the City*, Virginie Mamadouh and Anne van Wageningen, eds, Amsterdam University Press, Amsterdam, 2016, especially Part I, pp. 23–104; also Patricia Gosling and Nation Fitzroy, *Ethnic Amsterdam*, Vassalluci, Amsterdam, 2001.
35. Yamin Xu, Jefferson Wang and Yue Liu, 'These cities are the best connected in the world: What makes them so special?', World Economic Forum, 19 January 2022.
36. Benjamin R. Barber, *If Mayors Ruled the World: Dysfunctional Nations, Rising Cities*, Yale University Press, New Haven, CT, 2014, p. xxi.
37. Saskia Sassen, 'Locating Cities on Global Circuits', in *Global Networks: Linked Cities*, Saskia Sassen, ed., Routledge, London, 2002, p. 2.
38. Ibid. See also Ugo Rossi, *Cities in Global Capitalism*, Polity Press, Cambridge, 2017, pp. 2–18.
39. James Angel, 'New municipalism and the state: Remunicipalising energy in Barcelona, from prosaics to process', Antipode, Wiley Online Library, 2021;

Keir Milburn and Bertie Russell, 'Public-common partnerships: Building new circuits of collective ownership', Common Wealth, 27 June 2019.

40. Roman Krznaric, 'The Return of the City State (and the Slow Death of Nation States)', 1 January 2018; Sharon Chang, 'Return of the City State in 2050 – With Significant Upgrades'. Networks of cities within states are also highly institutionalized and active as manifested by the association of Italy's 8,000 mayors (ANCI), for instance. See 'Mayors call on govt to make masks obligatory outdoors', *ANSA*, 29 November 2021.

41. Eyck Freymann, *One Belt One Road: Chinese Power Meets the World*, Harvard University Press, Cambridge, MA, 2020.

42. 'The Silk Road', National Geographic Society.

43. Historians have pointed out that most colonial enterprises were preceded by the work of missionaries and traders, with state coming later only to formalize de facto acquisitions through traditional diplomatic means. See for example Ronald Hyam, *Understanding the British Empire*, Cambridge University Press, Cambridge, 2010; Thomas P. Cavanna, 'Coercion Unbound? China's Belt and Road Initiative', in *The Uses and Abuses of Weaponized Interdependence*, Daniel W. Drezner, Henry Farrell and Abraham L. Newman, eds, Brookings Institution Press, Washington, DC, 2021, pp. 221–38.

44. Markus Leif Sören Markert, *The Role of Non-State Actors in Foreign Policy Decision-Making Processes in the Non-Western World*, DPhil Thesis, University of Oxford, 2021, pp. 110–68.

45. Mette Eilstrup-Sangiovanni, 'Power and Purpose in Transgovernmental Networks: Insights from the Global Non-Proliferation Regime', in Avant and Westerwinter, *The New Power Politics*, pp. 131–67.

46. *European Union Power and Policy Making*, Jeremy Richardson, ed., Routledge, London, 2001, pp. 12–15; Christopher Hood, 'The Garbage Can Model of Organization: Describing a Condition or a Perspective Design Principle?', in *Organizing Political Institutions*, Morten Egeberg and Per Lægreid, eds, Scandinavia University Press, Oslo, 1999.

47. *Constitutional Change in the EU: From Uniformity to Flexibility?*, Gráinne de Búrca and Joanne Scott, eds, Hart, Oxford, 2000; Marlene Wind, 'The European Union as a Polycentric Polity: Returning to a Neo-medieval Europe?', in *European Constitutionalism Beyond the State*, J.H.H. Weiler and Marlene Wind, eds, Cambridge University Press, Cambridge, 2003, pp. 103–32.

48. Ferguson, *The Square and the Tower*, p. 422.

49. Russell Hotten, 'Ukraine conflict: What is Swift and why is banning Russia so significant?', *BBC News*, 4 May 2022; Dam Milmo, 'Anonymous: the hacker collective that has declared cyberwar on Russia', *Guardian*, 27 February 2022; Megan Cerullo, 'Elon Musk activates free SpaceX Starlink satellite internet service in Ukraine', *CBS News*, 28 February 2022; 'I.O.C. recommends barring athletes from Russia and Belarus', *New York Times*, 28 February 2022.

50. Anne-Marie Slaughter, *The Chessboard and the Web*, Yale University Press, New Haven, CT, 2017, p. 7.

51. 'Urban Agenda for the EU: Pact of Amsterdam', European Commission, 2016.

52. United Nations, 'Our Common Agenda: A Vision of the Future of Global Cooperation', UN Foundation, 2021.

53. In fact, networks also create hierarchies, although different than those created by states. See David Smith and Michael Timberlake, 'Hierarchies of Dominance among World Cities: A Network Approach', in Sassen, *Global Networks: Linked Cities*, pp. 117–41.

54. The following points draw from Milton L. Mueller, *Networks and States: The Global Politics of Internet Governance*, MIT Press, Cambridge, MA, 2010, pp. 4–5.

55. Darren Loucaides, 'Telegram: The digital battlefront between Russia and Ukraine', *Politico*, 10 March 2022; Stephen Warwick, 'How Russians are flocking to VPN apps as state censorship tightens', iMore.com, 5 March 2022.

56. Number of monthly active Facebook users worldwide as of 2nd quarter 2022, Statista.com.

57. Maarten Hajer, 'Policy without a Polity? Policy Analysis and the Institutional Void', *Policy Sciences*, 36, 2003, p. 175.

58. Juan J. Linz and Alfred Stepan, *Problems of Democratic Transition and Consolidation*, Johns Hopkins University Press, Baltimore, MD, 1979, p. 169.

59. Ralf Dahrendorf, 'The Challenge for Democracy', *Journal of Democracy*, 14/4, 2003, p. 106; and Juan J. Linz and Alfred C. Stepan, *Problems of Democratic Transition and Consolidation: Southern Europe, South America, and Post-Communist Europe*, Johns Hopkins University Press, Baltimore, MD, 1996.

60. See Chris Bickerton, *The European Union: A Citizen's Guide*, Penguin Books, London, 2016, pp. 219–30; Stéphanie Hennerre, Thomas Piketty, Guillaume Sacriste and Antoine Vauchez, *How to Democratize Europe*, Harvard University Press, Cambridge, MA, 2019, pp. 1–5.

61. John Keane, *Power and Humility: The Future of Monitory Democracy*, Cambridge University Press, Cambridge, 2018, p. 14.

62. See especially Robert A. Dahl, *On Democracy*, Yale University Press, New Haven, CT, 2000, pp. 7–25; Adam Przeworski, *Crises of Democracy*, Cambridge University Press, Cambridge, 2019, pp. 78–80; Robert Menasse, *Der Europäische Landbote*, Zsolnay Verlag, Vienna, 2012; Alessandro Pizzorno, 'Politics Unbound', in *Changing Boundaries of the Political: Essays on the Evolving Balance between the State and Society, Public and Private in Europe*, Charles S. Maier, ed., Cambridge University Press, Cambridge, 1987, pp. 27–62.

63. 'Global Parliamentary Report', Inter-Parliamentary Union, UNDP; Balázs Gyimesi, 'Trust in parliament', OECD, 11 February 2018.

64. All actors, including seemingly legitimate International Governmental Organizations and Non-Governmental Organizations, can behave deplorably. See for example Mayur Joshi, 'Money laundering through Indian NGOs: Indian NGOs and the risk of laundering', indiaforensic.com; Henry Zeffman, 'Charity sex scandal: UN staff "responsible for 60,000 rapes in a decade"', *The Times*, 14 February 2018.

65. This chiefly concerns such matters as logistical support, crime deterrence, intelligence gathering, peace-keeping and protection services. See for example 'Privatization of war', International Committee of the Red Cross, 11 December 2013, icrc.org. Also Wikipedia, List of private military contractors.

66. For instance, in 2022 financial networks were crucial in an effort to remove Russian banks from the messaging system that enables digital international

payments, the so-called SWIFT. See Claire Jones, 'The impact of throwing Russia out of Swift', *Financial Times*, 25 February 2022.

67. See Larry Winter Roeder and Albert Simard, *Diplomacy and Negotiation for Humanitarian NGOs: Humanitarian Solutions in the 21st Century*, Springer, New York, 2013, pp. 1–19.

68. Joseph S. Nye, Jr, *Soft Power: The Means to Success in World Politics*, Public Affairs, New York, 2004.

69. See Jan Kooiman, *Governing as Governance*, Sage, London, 2003.

70. However, an informal network called the Mont Pèlerin Society became the embryo of what its organizer, Friedrich Hayek, called the neoliberal movement. See Bruce Caldwell, *Mont Pèlerin 1947: Transcripts of the Founding Meeting of the Mont Pèlerin Society*, Hoover Institution, 2022; Mont Pèlerin Society, www.montpelerin.org.

71. Mark Bevir, *Governance: A Very Short Introduction*, Oxford University Press, Oxford, 2012, p. 5; Bevir, *Democratic Governance*, pp. 82–5.

72. R.A.W. Rhodes, 'Policy Network Analysis', in *The Oxford Handbook of Public Policy*, Michael Moran, Martin Rein and Robert E. Goodin, eds, Oxford University Press, Oxford, 2008, pp. 425–47.

73. *Debating Governance: Authority, Steering, and Democracy*, Jon Pierre, ed., Oxford University Press, Oxford, 2000.

74. Nowotny, *An Orderly Mess*.

75. See Yochai Benkler, *The Wealth of Networks: How Social Production Transforms Markets and Freedom*, Yale University Press, New Haven, CT, 2006.

76. Mueller, *Networks and States*, pp. 254–71.

77. Soft law privileges informal agreements and contracts instead of top-down regulation, and information or persuasion instead of repression. See for example Francis Snyder, 'Soft Law and Institutional Practice in the European Community', in *The Construction of Europe: Essays in Honor of Emile Noël*, Stephen Martin, ed., Kluwer, Deventer, 1994, pp. 197–227.

78. Helen Margetts, Peter John, Scott Hale and Taha Yasseri, *Political Turbulence: How Social Media Shape Collective Action*, Princeton University Press, Princeton, NJ, 2016, p. 217.

79. Mikkel Flyverbom, *The Power of Networks: Organizing the Global Politics of the Internet*, Edward Elgar Publishing, Cheltenham, 2011, p. 160.

80. In July 2018, over 160 AI companies and 2,400 individual researchers from across the globe signed an open pledge promising to never develop such weapons. See: https://futureoflife.org/lethal-autonomous-weapons-pledge/.

81. See Christopher Hill, *The National Interest in Question: Foreign Policy in Multicultural Societies*, Oxford University Press, Oxford, 2013.

82. Keane, *The New Despotism*, p. 254. Also Margetts, John, Hale and Yasseri, *Political Turbulence*.

8 RENEWING THE COSMOPOLIS

1. Rooney, *About Time*, p. 6.

2. See for example Ulrich Beck, *German Europe*, Polity Press, Cambridge, 2013.

3. Michael Zürn, *A Theory of Global Governance: Authority, Legitimacy, and Contestation*, Oxford University Press, Oxford, 2018; Andrew Hurrell, *On Global Order: Power, Values, and the Constitution of International Society*, Oxford University Press, Oxford, 2007.

4. I wrote about the European case in Jan Zielonka, *Is the EU Doomed?*, Polity Press, Cambridge, 2014. For a harsh critique of the UN: Dore Gold, *Tower of Babble: How the United Nations Has Fueled Global Chaos*, Crown Publishing Group, New York, 2004.

5. Gavin Jacobson, 'Why *Children of Men* haunts the present moment', *New Statesman*, 22 July 2020.

6. Rafi Letzter, 'Will the US Be Able to Stop Russia's New Arsenal of Missile Defense-Piercing Nukes?', *Live Science*, 4 March 2018; Selvaggia Lucarelli, 'Di fronte alla guerra in Ucraina e all'escalation, rivendico il diritto di tutti ad avere paura' ['In the face of the war in Ukraine and the escalation, I claim the right of everyone to be afraid'], *Domani*, editorial, 3 May 2022.

7. Srećko Horvat, *After the Apocalypse*, Polity Press, Cambridge, 2021, p. 2.

8. Tadeusz Konwicki, *A Minor Apocalypse*, Farrar, Straus and Giroux, New York, 1983, p. 43. Interestingly, the Ukrainian novels depicting their country, especially Donbas, before the Russian invasion of 2022 are equally ironic. See especially Wołodymyr Rafiejenko's *The Longest Times*, published in Ukrainian (and Polish): Володомир Рафєєнко, *Довгі часи*, Видавництво Старого Лева, Lviv, 2017; Tomáš Forró, *Donbas: Wedding Apartment in the Hotel War*, published in Slovak (and Polish): *Donbas: svadobný apartmán v hoteli Vojna*, N. Press, Bratislava, 2019.

9. Archie Brown, *Seven Years that Changed the World: Perestroika in Perspective*, Oxford University Press, Oxford, 2007.

10. See Hannah Arendt, *Between Past and Future*, Viking, New York, 1961; Karl Popper, *The Open Society and its Enemies*, 2 vols, Routledge, London, 1945; Isaiah Berlin, *Liberty*, Oxford University Press, Oxford, 2002.

11. John Dewey, *The Quest for Certainty: A Study of the Relation of Knowledge and Action*, Minton, Balch & Company, New York, 1929, p. 223. See also Keane, 'Thoughts on Uncertainty'.

12. Hartmut Rosa, *The Uncontrollability of the World*, Polity Press, Cambridge, 2020, p. 116.

13. Global Parliament of Mayors, https://globalparliamentofmayors.org/.

14. Parliament of the World's Religions, https://parliamentofreligions.org/.

15. UN Parliamentary Assembly, Supporters of the campaign for a UN Parliamentary Assembly, unpacampaign.org.

16. David Held, 'Democracy: From City-States to a Cosmopolitan Order?', in *Prospects for Democracy*, David Held, ed., Polity Press, Cambridge, 1993, pp. 13–52.

17. See for example *The Future of Representative Democracy*, Sonia Alonso, John Keane and Wolfgang Merkel, eds, Cambridge University Press, Cambridge, 2011.

18. John Keane, *Democracy and Media Decadence*, Cambridge University Press, Cambridge, 2013, p. 81.

19. International Labour Organization, 'The Nobel Peace Prize, 1969, Facts and Motivation', https://www.nobelprize.org/prizes/peace/1969/labour/facts/.

20. Herman van den Bosch, 'Barcelona and Madrid: Forerunners in e-governance', Amsterdam Smart City, 23 September 2021.
21. 'Citizens to decide how to improve neighbourhoods with the first participatory budget', Info Barcelona, Barcelona City Council, 3 February 2020.
22. David Van Reybrouck, *Against Elections: The Case for Democracy*, Seven Stories Press, London, 2018.
23. Konwicki, *A Minor Apocalypse*, p. 52.
24. T.S. Eliot, 'East Coker', *Four Quartets*, Faber & Faber, London, 2001.

FURTHER READING

This is a selection of readings which may help the reader to explore some of the topics discussed in this book. I have tried to offer a mixture of fairly recent popular and academic books. Choices made are personal and therefore highly biased, and they are all in English, which is a serious limitation. However, I hope the selected books offer an appetizing intellectual menu. Enjoy your reading!

POLITICS OF TIME

Elizabeth F. Cohen, *The Political Value of Time: Citizenship, Duration, and Democratic Justice*, Cambridge University Press, Cambridge, 2018.

Klaus H. Goetz, ed., *The Oxford Handbook of Time and Politics*, Oxford University Press, Oxford, 2019.

Robert E. Goodin, James Mahmud Rice, Antti Parpo and Lina Erikson, *Discretionary Time: A New Measure of Freedom*, Cambridge University Press, Cambridge, 2008.

Michael K. MacKenzie, *Future Publics: Democracy, Deliberation, and Future-Regarding Collective Action*, Oxford University Press, Oxford, 2021.

David Rooney, *About Time: A History of Civilization in Twelve Clocks*, Norton, New York, 2021.

POLITICS OF SPACE

James Crawford, *The Edge of the Plain: How Borders Make and Break Our World*, Canongate, Edinburgh, 2022).

Charles S. Maier, *Once within Borders: Territories of Power, Wealth, and Belonging since 1500*, Belknap Press, Cambridge, MA, 2016.

Paulina Ochoa Espejo, *On Borders: Territories, Legitimacy and the Rights of Place*, Oxford University Press, Oxford, 2020.

FURTHER READING

A. John Simmons, *Boundaries of Authority*, Oxford University Press, Oxford, 2016.

Pieter de Wilde, Ruud Koopmans, Wolfgang Merkel, Oliver Strijbis and Michael Zürn, eds, *The Struggle over Borders: Cosmopolitanism and Communitarianism*, Cambridge University Press, Cambridge, 2019.

DEMOCRACY IN CRISIS

Christopher J. Bickerton and Carlo Invernizzi Accetti, *Technopopulism: The New Logic of Democratic Politics*, Oxford University Press, Oxford, 2021.

Steven Levitsky and Daniel Ziblatt, *How Democracies Die*, Crown, New York; Viking, UK, 2018.

Adam Przeworski, *Crises of Democracy*, Cambridge University Press, Cambridge, 2019.

David Runciman, *How Democracy Ends*, Basic Books, New York, 2018.

Wojciech Sadurski, *A Pandemic of Populists*, Cambridge University Press, Cambridge, 2022.

CAPITALISM IN CRISIS

Jürgen Kocka, *Capitalism: A Short History*, Princeton University Press, Princeton, NJ, 2016.

Robert B. Reich, *The System: Who Rigged It, How We Fix It*, Knopf Publishing, New York, 2020.

Michael J. Sandel, *What Money Can't Buy: The Moral Limits of Markets*, Farrar, Straus and Giroux, New York, 2012.

Joseph E. Stiglitz, *Globalization and its Discontents*, Norton, New York, 2002.

Wolfgang Streeck, *How Will Capitalism End?*, Verso, London, 2016.

THE WORLD IN CRISIS

Niall Ferguson, *Doom: The Politics of Catastrophe*, Allen Lane, New York, 2021.

Paul G. Harris, *Pathologies of Climate Governance*, Cambridge University Press, Cambridge, 2021.

John Keane, *The New Despotism*, Harvard University Press, Cambridge, MA, 2020.

Mark Leonard, *The Age of Unpeace: How Connectivity Causes Conflict*, Penguin, London, 2022.

Branco Milanovic, *Global Inequality: A New Approach for the Age of Globalization*, Belknap Press, Cambridge, MA, 2018.

Saskia Sassen, *Expulsions: Brutality and Complexity in the Global Economy*, Harvard University Press, Cambridge, MA, 2014.

HIGH vs SLOW SPEED

Robert Colvile, *The Great Acceleration: How the World is Getting Faster, Faster*, Bloomsbury Publishing, London, 2016.

FURTHER READING

Jonathan Crary, *24/7: Late Capitalism and the Ends of Sleep*, Verso, London, 2013.

Danny Dorling, *Slowdown: The End of the Great Acceleration – and Why It's Good for the Planet, the Economy, and Our Lives*, Yale University Press, London, 2020.

Hartmut Rosa and William E. Scheuerman, eds, *High-Speed Society: Social Acceleration, Power and Modernity*, Penn State University Press, University Park, PA, 2009.

Judy Wajcman, *Pressed for Time: The Acceleration of Life in Digital Capitalism*, University of Chicago Press, Chicago, IL, 2015.

UNBOUNDING vs RE-BOUNDING

Alexander Betts and Paul Collier, *Refugee: Transforming a Broken Refugee System*, Allen Lane, London, 2017.

Daniel W. Drezner, Henry Farrell and Abraham L. Newman, eds, *The Uses and Abuses of Weaponized Interdependence*, Brookings Institution Press, Washington, DC, 2021.

Andrew Geddes, *Governing Migration beyond the State: Europe, North America, and Southeast Asia in a Global Context*, Oxford University Press, Oxford, 2021.

Dani Rodrik, *The Globalization Paradox*, Oxford University Press, Oxford, 2011.

Saskia Sassen, *Territory, Authority and Rights: From Medieval to Global Assemblages*, Princeton University Press, Princeton, NJ, 2006.

CONTESTED MEMORIES

Helmut Anheier and Yudhishthir Raj Isar, eds, *Heritage, Memory & Identity*, Sage, London, 2011.

James M. Banner, Jr, *The Ever-Changing Past: Why All History Is Revisionist History*, Yale University Press, London, 2021.

Małgorzata Pakier and Bo Stråth, eds, *A European Memory? Contested Histories and Politics of Remembrance*, Berghahn Books, New York, 2010.

Paul Ricoeur, *Memory, History, Forgetting*, University of Chicago Press, Chicago, IL, 2004.

Vladimir Tismaneanu, ed., *Remembrance, History, and Justice: Coming to Terms with Traumatic Pasts in Democratic Societies*, Central European University Press, Budapest, 2015.

CONTESTED TECHNOLOGIES

Nick Bostrom, *Superintelligence: Paths, Dangers, Strategies*, Oxford University Press, Oxford, 2014.

Martin Ford, *Rise of the Robots: Technology and the Threat of a Jobless Future*, Basic Books, New York, 2015.

Carl Benedict Frey, *The Technology Trap: Capital, Labour and Power in the Age of Automation*, Princeton University Press, Princeton, NJ, 2019.

Helga Nowotny, *In AI We Trust: Power, Illusion and Control of Predictive Algorithms*, Polity Press, Cambridge, 2021.

Justin E.H. Smith, *The Internet Is Not What You Think It Is: A History, a Philosophy, a Warning*, Princeton University Press, Princeton, NJ, 2022.

FURTHER READING

INNOVATIVE GOVERNANCE

Deborah Avant and Oliver Westerwinter, *The New Power Politics: Networks and Transnational Security Governance*, Oxford University Press, Oxford, 2016.

Benjamin R. Barber, *If Mayors Ruled the World: Dysfunctional Nations, Rising Cities*, Yale University Press, New Haven, CT, and London, 2013.

Mark Bevir, *Democratic Governance*, Princeton University Press, Princeton, NJ, 2010.

William Hall, Anthony McDonnell and Jim O'Neill, *Superbugs: An Arms Race against Bacteria*, Harvard University Press, Cambridge, MA, 2018.

Anne-Marie Slaughter, *The Chessboard and the Web*, Yale University Press, New Haven, CT, 2017.

DESIGNING THE FUTURE

Chris Benner and Manuel Pastor, *Solidarity Economics: Why Mutuality of Movements Matter*, Polity Press, Cambridge, 2021.

Danny Cullenward and David G. Victor, *Making Climate Policy Work*, Polity Press, Cambridge, 2020.

Iñigo González-Ricoy and Axel Gosseries, eds, *Institutions for Future Generations*, Oxford University Press, Oxford, 2016.

Yuval Noah Harari, *Homo Deus: A Brief History of Tomorrow*, Vintage, London, 2017.

John Keane, *Power and Humility: The Future of Monitory Democracy*, Cambridge University Press, Cambridge, 2018.

Parag Khanna, *Connectography: Mapping the Future of Global Civilization*, Random House, New York, 2016.

Vili Lehdonvirta, *Cloud Empires: How Digital Platforms Are Overtaking the State and How We Can Regain Control*, MIT Press, Boston, 2022.

William MacAskill, *What We Owe the Future: A Million-Year View*, Basic Books, New York, 2022.

Mark Maslin, *How to Save Our Planet*, Penguin, London, 2021.

Paul Mason, *Postcapitalism: A Guide to Our Future*, Farrar, Straus and Giroux, New York, 2015.

Graham Smith, *Can Democracy Safeguard the Future?*, Polity Press, Cambridge, 2021.

Ben Tarnoff, *Internet for the People: The Fight for Our Digital Future*, Verso, London, 2022.

Michael Zürn, *A Theory of Global Governance: Authority, Legitimacy and Contestation*, Oxford University Press, Oxford, 2018.

INDEX

INDEX

INDEX

INDEX